WORLD WAR II
LONG ISLAND

·············· ★ ··············

The Homefront in Nassau and Suffolk

CHRISTOPHER VERGA

THE
History
PRESS

Published by The History Press
Charleston, SC
www.historypress.com

First published 2021

Manufactured in the United States

ISBN 9781467147187

Library of Congress Control Number: 2020945749

CONTENTS

ACKNOWLEDGEMENTS

No one person can own or monopolize the history they write or interpret. The gatekeeper to our history lies in the collective efforts of a community to keep it alive. Whomever we recognize as heroes or villains are defined by the impacts they had on the communities they represented. World War II and Long Island had many fronts domestically, town/county historical societies and local libraries have encapsulated the contributions of Long Islanders' World War II legacies for generations to come.

This book would have not been possible without the help and support of the many people who tirelessly work to preserve this history through image collections and interviews. Smithtown Library's Veterans Oral History Project was essential in re-creating the veterans' experiences prior to the war and coming home from the war. I would like to thank Julia Blum of the Cradle of Aviation of Nassau County for granting me access to the images of old Mitchel Field. I also want to thank Paul Infranco and Melanie Cardone-Leather of Longwood Public Library for their images and background information on Camp Upton. I would like to express my gratitude for the images of the Tuskegee Airmen and access to the internment camp letters that was provided to me by Dr. Geri Solomon and Hofstra University Special Collections. These images and documents were the backbone of my retelling of an almost forgotten history. I would like to extend special recognition to all the local historians I consulted with at the Bay Shore Historical Society, Nassau County

Historical Services, Suffolk County Historical Society and Fire Island Lighthouse Historical Society.

Most of all, I would like to thank all who served overseas and domestically during World War II. This book is an attempt to not only honor your efforts but to preserve it for generations to come. With our collective efforts, we will prevent those who died in service to their country from dying a second death of being forgotten.

PRE–WORLD WAR II LONG ISLAND

Pre–World War II Long Island was unrecognizable when compared to the current landscape, which is dotted with massive suburban developments, strip malls and complex parkways and expressways. Nassau and Suffolk Counties had long-ingrained biases, norms and their own economies for generations, but unlike the generational buildup of a regional identity, Long Island's full modernization into the twentieth century took less than five years. This modernization of Long Island defined the area's current economic and social viability by 1945. The Long Island of the 1930s and 1940s, which comprised Nassau and Suffolk Counties, had a fraction of its current population of almost three million. In the decades prior to 1940, homes in many communities were referred to by family names instead of by street and number. Throughout both counties, traditional nineteenth-century dirt farm roads were the main transportation routes. East of Rockville Center, the most densely populated areas were the farthest South and North Shore communities, such as Bay Shore, Patchogue, Freeport and Huntington Village, which had an industry built around commercial fishing, shellfish harvesting, boat building and textile mills. The total population of Nassau County in 1930 was 303,053, which rose to 406,748 in 1940. Suffolk County, the least populated of the two, had a population of 161,055 in 1930 and 197,355 by 1940. The land masses of both counties were made up of potato farms, landing strips for hobby aviators and the large Gilded Age estates of some of America's richest families. Similar to other small agricultural areas of the time, both counties had an isolationist mentality toward New York City, immigration and foreign affairs, which made most residents generally opposed to any construction project that would integrate eastern communities onto an exit ramp for a parkway or expressway system.

Foreign isolationism within Long Island was fueled through the open wounds of the World War I. America lost a total of 116,516 people to World War I. From that number, Nassau and Suffolk Counties, which made up 108 communities and villages, lost 347 men. Adding to the losses from World War I, demobilizing soldiers brought home with them a new strand of influenza that was later named the Spanish flu. This pandemic killed an estimated 100 million people worldwide and almost 675,000 Americans. The pandemic had patient zeros coming from local military bases in every state. Across Long Island, demobilized soldiers coming home from Europe were stationed in large numbers at Camp Upton Brookhaven and Mitchel Field Hempstead. Camp Upton was the first hot zone cluster of the Spanish flu for Long Island and New York City. By October 1918, Camp Upton had 3,050 cases of a flu that was causing a bacterial pneumonia. With the new cases, little to no action was taken by military officials to isolate the people showing symptoms. These demobilized soldiers were allowed to interact in local surrounding communities. Across Suffolk and Nassau Counties, towns burdened with the flu were levied with the expenses of prevention and care. Day-to-day life was stalled, with school closings that lasted weeks at a time and other popular social events canceled in efforts to slow the spread of the flu. Before these increasing flu numbers and preventions across Long Island were reported to proper military authorities, many of the Camp Upton and Mitchel Field soldiers headed home to the densely populated New York City. Parades with thousands of people welcomed home the soldiers, and overcrowded social gatherings celebrated soldiers with tales of how they braved the face of death—all without knowing they were about to face an invisible death.

Within a short time, an estimated 30,000 New York City residents were killed by the pandemic that struck in three deadly waves. Fortunately for New York, it did not suffer the devastation of other cities and states, like Philadelphia, which had 16,000 deaths out of a total population of 500,000 (this was a greater mortality rate, as New York City had 30,000 deaths with a population of 5.6 million people). Headlines plagued the local papers across Long Island, as they shared the horrors of the flu pandemic, stories of the war and commentaries on returning to an isolationist policy globally.

Building on the horrors of the pandemic and war causalities, Long Island was hit by a postwar recession. Following World War I, a labor glut

Westbury's World War I veterans in 1920. *Courtesy of the Historical Society of the Westburys Photograph Archive.*

played out between the locals and the new Italian, Jewish, eastern European immigrants and thousands of African Americans fleeing the South for jobs. The results of this influx of workers and a bad economy were lowered wages and unemployment across Nassau and Suffolk Counties. In the midst of the falling wages and labor glut, Long Island was going through a drastic demographic change due to the new immigration. The Ku Klux Klan experienced a surge in membership and expanded membership chapters across New York and Long Island. The goal of the expanded Klan membership was to wage successful campaigns in local elections, which would give control of political offices to pro-Klan candidates that would make laws to restrict building Catholic churches and further isolate minority populations. False newspapers circulated by the Ku Klux Klan flooded local Long Island communities more than real newspapers. The Klan paper *Vigilance* reported that New York governor Al Smith was conscripting to make America a colony of the Roman Catholic Church. Other Klan-based news sources, such as the *Kourier Magazine*, declared in July 1927 that the "Catholic Church teaches disloyalty to America, which pulled America into World War I." Another falsehood detailed by local Klan papers was a "potential invasion of America by the elected Catholic governor Alfred Smith, who [was] purposely promoting the breakdown of American values."[1] This media spurred distrust and anxiety against all immigrants and minorities in Long Island communities. The local outcome was that one in seven Long Islanders became Klan members. Local store owners and businesses began hanging signs that read TWAK (trade only with a Klansman) to demonstrate solidarity with local Klan members and their willingness to hire only White Anglo-Saxon Protestants. As Klan membership grew, ritual parades of Klan members took place while Catholic churches and synagogues were in service in an effort to intermediate the congregations. With the fake news and rise of radicalism, locals' global views were being built around staying isolated from global affairs and the thought that any interaction globally would be a threat to the day-to-day lives of local Long Islanders. But to further complicate the rise of radicalism, bigotry and falling wages, a sudden crash of the stock market wiped out generational and superficial wealth of Long Island's most powerful people.

On October 24, 1929, the stock market crashed, and the state New York, which prided itself with the Latin phrase *excelsior*, meaning always rising, fell. Over nine thousand banks failed, with more than the entire cost of World War I lost in the stock market within a week. Throughout the country, unemployment spiked to 25 percent. These economic effects hit the everyday people across Long Island. Locals who worked on large estates for America's wealthiest people found themselves unemployed, homeless and wandering from town to town for stability. The growing aviation sector along the Hempstead Plains, the pride of Nassau County, became thousands of acres of barren thicket bushes. The western parts of Nassau County and eastern Queens by Thurston's Creek became known as "Hungry Harbor" due to the squatter shacks that were erected by locals who lost their homes to foreclosures. The homeless residents of New York City, scared due the rumors of starvation deaths, flooded out to Nassau and Suffolk farms to seek employment. Dozens of hungry people dug through harvested potato fields to see if any small potatoes had been left behind. Money became scarce; even farms that had been owned by families for generations broke down into a local economy based on bartering.

To further add to the economic hardships of Long Island, on September 21, 1938, Long Island experienced one of its largest hurricanes on record.

Vacationing resort communities that were economic staples for South Shore towns, including the Hamptons and Bay Shore, which were economically stable during the depression, were soon ground zero for another wave of economic disaster. Fire Island, a large barrier island that comprises seventeen towns, was a patchwork of booming seasonal communities that shared a lot of tourist revenue with Bay Shore. The largest towns on the island, such as Saltaire, were leveled and suffered multiple deaths. In West Hampton, an entire movie theater, where a few people took shelter from the storm, was washed out into the ocean. The deaths were estimated to number fifty, but the fear of vacationing near the water shut down resort communities for the following decade. But the worst economic impact was the destruction of the area's all-natural shellfish beds. Over three thousand people became unemployed overnight due to the oyster beds being washed out into the ocean.

Long Island was fragmented through ethnic, racial and economic divides. The rise of racist groups such as the Ku Klux Klan further broke down locals into separate societies within one town. With a combined population of four hundred thousand, Long Island was more divided than a country of 135 million. For more than two decades, the population retreated into an isolationist view of the world and pushed back with force on anything that challenged it. Local economies endured by breaking away from a national economy to become their own autonomous states within New York. The process to mobilize such an area for a global war that depended on the workforce, resources and loyalty of its people was highly unlikely to be successful. The lack of trust among the locals and the lack of a unified vision for America were far removed for Long Islanders. But in facing the global realities that came crashing down on Long Island, the historic biases that created institutionalized racism and the desire for isolation in world politics were challenged. How did Long Island become the arsenal for democracy? How did Long Island become home to a counterintelligence ring that gave America an advantage in the D-Day invasion? How did Long Island enlist volunteers to become some of the bravest fighters in World War II? What was the drastic shift that made Long Island a hub for winning the war? How did Long Islanders build a shared vision around defined rights and universal virtues? And most of all, what global reasonability did Long Island have as a region to take out fascism? Long Island before World War II was known to be estranged to its own region, but in less than five years, it became a region of global citizens that housed the first United Nations in Lake Success, Nassau County.

1.

DEFENDING THE HOMEFRONT FROM THREATS OUTSIDE AND WITHIN

Prior to the declared war, Long Island was fighting a two-front war with Germany. One front came from threats within, such as spy rings and Nazi sympathizers, and the other front came from an invasion abroad. Forced to be shrouded in secrecy, workers in various manufacturing companies were being monitored by the FBI. This was not paranoia but a response to spies ingrained in the fabric of suburban communities and protected by a substantial population of residents with antiwar and Nazi-sympathizing sentiments. In 1941, as the war drew closer, dangers of the spy networks and Nazi naval abilities became public, and many locals saw these activities as acts of war. Domestic Nazi supporters became outliers to the greater population as residents suffered the anxiety of oncoming war. A vast majority of Long Islanders, despite their differences in race social or economic class, became unified against a shared enemy. This shared enemy kept most Long Islanders living on the edge for fear of invasion or state-sponsored terrorist attacks, but the biggest concerns were the gaps in providing security on the homefront through a fast-growing wartime manufacturing industry.

On Saturday, June 28, 1941, Everett Roeder of Merrick was relaxing after a long week at work. But this June morning relaxation was short-lived. Black cars carrying FBI agents pulled onto the front lawn of 210 Smith Street in Merrick and stormed Roeder's front door with guns drawn. In a short time, Roeder was taken away in cuffs and spent sixteen years in federal prison. Roeder had two sons and a daughter whom neighbors described as very quiet; they never spoke to anyone.[2] At work, Roeder was a top engineer with Sperry Gyroscope Company in Garden City. The projects he worked on included bombsights, long-range guns for planes and cutting-edge autopilot technology. Similar to dozens of other Long Island companies, Sperry Gyroscope Company was hiring thousands of workers at a rapid speed—with little to no security clearances—in order to fill the innovation hub for aircraft technology.

All of the Sperry Gyroscope Company's projects were considered confidential and were produced exclusively for the United States Defense Department. America was on the cusp of war, which made preparation of any military production a priority. The once-sluggish aircraft factories across Long Island that operated at austerity levels due to the grips of the Great Depression had a dramatic shift. Within a few short years, aircraft manufacturers had an exclusive customer with a blank check: the government. New Yorkers across the state took advantage of the wealth of the aircraft manufacturing industry, but other groups took notice of the industry's success, including Nazi Germany. Roeder, who lived and worked in the center of this technological field, became an asset for intelligence whom the Nazi's utilized. By the early 1940s, the Luftwaffe fighter planes were equipped with autopilot and other technologies that Sperry's was innovating to give the American Air Corps an advantage. This intelligence provided by Roeder and other spies gave the Nazis had an equal footing in combat.

Everett Roeder was part of one of the two large Nazi Spy rings that preyed on Long Island's technological sector. Duquesne Spy Ring, which Roeder was part of, comprised thirty-three operatives who mainly worked in the New York City and Long Island area. The New York German Consulate recruited the thirty-three spies. The recruited worked for companies such as Westinghouse Electric, Bendix Aviation, Pan American Airways and Ford Motor Company. Each spy was well compensated and communicated the secrets they obtained through shortwave radio stations to Nazi representatives. The two shortwave stations were located in the Bronx and Centerport, Suffolk County, Long Island. These radio transmissions communicated secrets and drop-off and meet-up points for exchanging physical blueprints, models and prototypes of instruments that could further the Nazi war effort.[3] Rene Mezenen flew clipper planes for Pan American Airways and transported the acquired physical materials to Nazi representatives in Europe for pick up. The spy ring was such a success that Germany started to share their network with Japan. Roeder, who later became known as Carr on the shortwave radio transmissions, provided some of the most restrictive secrets of American airline technology. The Japanese, in an effort to further build up their air force, requested intelligence into the Sperry military projects. Lieutenant Takeo Ezima of the Japanese command collaborated directly with Roeder on what technical advancements their air force was in need of.[4] This network operated for approximately one year until it was neutralized on June 30, 1941.

While Roeder and the Duquesne spy ring were making gains for the Nazi cause in intelligence theft, a group of Nazi sympathizers formed a spy and sabotage ring. The ring was organized across Long Island and New York City with the goal of causing damage to local military bases and shipping centers in an effort to make them inoperative, while other members were to gather intelligence on the Republic Airline factory's new technologies. The head of this ring was Karl Schlueter, who was considered a traveling agent in the Nazi intelligence service. Known active members of the ring included Otto Voss of Floral Park, who was employed by Republic Aircraft Company in Farmingdale; Erich Glaser, an enlisted private who was stationed at Mitchel Field Hempstead; Gustave Rumrich, an AWOL army soldier; and Johanna Hofmann, who worked on German Ocean liners that were coming in and out of New York City ports.

This network, unlike the Duquesne ring, achieved very little success. Schlueter's role as the head of the ring was to draw in willing collaborators; the intelligence gathered from collaborators was transported to Germany by Johanna Hofmann. In later testimony against Schlueter, it was discovered his plans evolved from gathering aircraft manufacturing secrets to perfecting the production of counterfeit White House stationery, forging President Roosevelt's signature and obtaining plans from the navy yard for the new aircraft carriers.[5] The end of this spy ring came abruptly when the identity of the spies became known due to informants. Once his cover was exposed, Karl Schlueter tried to flee America on the ocean liner *Columbus*, which was docked at Ellis Island. Following his arrest, Schlueter received twenty years in prison; Voss got six years, Glasser two years, Hofmann four years and Gustave Rumrich, in exchange for his testimony against Schlueter, got the reduced sentence of two years.

The testimony given by Rumrich disclosed one common theme between both spy rings: all or most of the members had some form of connection to the German American Bund. Fritz Kuhn established the National German American Bund in ethnically German communities across Long Island and New Jersey. At its peak, the Bund had twenty-five thousand members. The

1936 founding guidelines of the original chapters said the organization was meant to promote the compatibility of German values and Americanization.

Following World War I, Germany was held responsible for the war and forced to pay full reparations. Covering the cost of the war and weak leadership in Germany created the perfect conditions for a rise in nationalism. German nationalism later evolved into Nazism, which was exported to ethnically German areas across the world. As German nationalism became Nazism and expanded across Europe, membership soared within the German American Bund. This membership growth led to the 1936 principles of Americanism shifting to antisemitism and Hitlerism. In promoting these causes, the Bund formed alliances with other extreme organizations, such as the Christian Front and the Protestant Civic Welfare Federation. Both of these groups participated in Bund rallies and shared antisemitic and antiwar views. To gather more members, the Bund, Christian Front and Protestant Civic Federation distributed propaganda across the economically devastated areas of New York City and Long Island. These groups published propaganda that promoted the antisemitic conspiracy of an, "international Jewish clique, which rewrote the constitution of the German Republic to enslave the 68 million German Christians economically and socially. And this group would do the same thing here if German people and other Prostates do not fight back."[6] With the pro-Nazi principles installed, the Bund and its allies supported state and federal candidates who had shared the same views and later would become a major fundraising division for foreign Nazi causes.

The German Bund and its alliances became visible to the general public on February 20, 1939. That night, the Bund leased out Madison Square Garden for a rally that celebrated George Washington's birthday in an effort to reflect how the Nazis' values could be compatible with America. During the rally, guest speakers warned of a Jewish threat and denounced President Franklin Roosevelt's decision to support England. The total number of attendees from the Bund was estimated to be twenty-two thousand, but the groups that protested the rally outside were estimated to number fifty-two thousand. The protesters included Jewish people, anti-Nazi groups and Socialist Workers Party members. The emotionally charged counterprotest remained peaceful, and only thirteen people were arrested.

The images of Nazis marching into Madison Square Garden to argue real American values became ingrained in every newsreel throughout the country. However, the size of this rally was dwarfed by Camp Siegfried in Yaphank. Camp Siegfried was the center for promoting Nazi values and

A bungalow next to Camp Siegfried displaying its support for the Nazis. *Courtesy of Longwood Library, Bayles Local History Room and Photograph Archives.*

raising money for Hitler in America. Fritz Kuhn petitioned Hitler for Nazi textbooks and uniforms for attendees of the camp. The shipping company used to deliver the uniforms, books and other supplies from Nazi Germany to Camp Siegfried was Remle Carlton Company, which was based in New York City. This company was also a benefactor that helped bankroll Bund rallies within the camp. During an average German Day celebration in the late 1930s, the camp had as many as forty thousand attendees, with two thousand uniformed Nazi storm troopers to keep order.[7] As families arrived at the camp, parents were encouraged to purchase Nazi war bonds, and children were taken for paramilitary exercises. During paramilitary exercises, children were given daggers and told to repeat the horrific phrase: "When Jewish blood drips from the knife, then will the German people prosper."[8] Fundraising, combined with military rituals, netted over $123,000 for the Nazi war machine through thousands of donations from loyalists to Hitler. While people attended these camp rallies, it is believed that German consulate lawyers and other diplomats scouted people who they felt were valuable for future spy rings.

This page and opposite: The German Bund home base and fundraising retreat Camp Siegfried Yaphank in Suffolk County. Attendees learned about antisemitism, racial superiority and other Nazism ideals. The camp raised as much as $120,000 in one summer for the promotion of Nazi causes throughout Europe. *Courtesy of Longwood Library, Bayles Local History Room and Photograph Archives.*

Members of the Bund who worked in aviation or at the shipyard or who were active American military members were top picks when expanding the network of Nazi spy rings. The actions of the camp attracted very little attention from locals and was seen as a summer camp until America got closer to joining World War II. In response to the media attention of an aggressive Germany, the Bund shifted its message from being pro-Hitler to being anti-Marxist. The camp also refrained from calling the country Nazi Germany; instead, it referred it as the "New Germany."[9] But no matter how the Bund remarketed its ideals, public opinion had shifted as Nazi Germany became more aggressive. The concern of an aggressive Nazi power drew the concerns of the FBI and the New York State Attorney General's Office.

In late 1938 and early 1939, the FBI started to track Fritz Kuhn's money transfers in and out of the country. According to FBI records, Kuhn was regularly meeting with Nazi commanders and Nazi intelligence officers in a building referred to as the Brown House in Munich throughout 1937.[10] Tracking the Bund finances drew even more concern throughout 1939 due to money being traced from fundraisers that originated from Camp Siegfried, which were distributed among Nazi Agents in Austria, Poland and Czechoslovakia.[11] Domestically, German American Bund funds were financing a "keep America Neutral" campaign, which was traced back to Nazi foreign operatives. The domestic campaign included newspaper advertisements and political donations. The FBI accumulated the intelligence against Kuhn and Long Island Bund leadership and slowly built a naturalization case, but in the New York State Attorney General's Office, they wanted faster results. Encouraged by the need to acquire the Bund membership rolls and all political connections, New York State assistant district attorney Lindsay Henry filed charges against the directors of Camp Siegfried for violating the New York civil rights law. The section 55 of the civil rights law required organizations to file membership rolls with the state. The Bund, understanding access to the rolls could jeopardize all connections, kept the names of its donors and members secret.

The case was to be heard in the Bay Shore district court on Main Street (present-day Siben & Siben Law Office). The defendants were Ernst Mueller, Henry Wolfgang, Bruno Haehnel, Herman Schwarzman, Aldo Bielefeld and Henry Hauck, and they were brought in and arraigned with crowds of onlookers watching as they marched in Nazi military uniforms into the court. After the arraignment, the assistant district attorney realized the court facilities could not accommodate the crowds. The case was moved

This page: Members and visitors to Camp Siegfried in militaristic exercises. *Courtesy of the Nassau County Photograph Archive.*

Members of the German Bund on trial in Bay Shore. *Courtesy of the Nassau County Photograph Archive.*

to Riverhead, and the preceding judge was Barron Hill. After refusing to cooperate with disclosing the membership rolls in return for reduced or dropped charges, all six men were found guilty. The sentences for all six members included one year in jail and $500 fines for each person.

Unfortunately, the convictions of the six camp leaders were reversed, but top officials were brought up on embezzlement and fraud charges. In the early 1940s, the FBI had documentation that showed Fritz Kuhn had embezzled $14,548 from the Bund, and the FBI shared this documentation with the New York State Attorney General's Office. The day New York attorney general Thomas Dewy announced formal charges, Kuhn fled the state. While driving across stateliness in a stolen car, local police in New Jersey arrested Kuhn and his associates. When he was brought back to New York, Kuhn was convicted of tax evasion and embezzlement and was sentenced to two to five years in prison in late 1939. Following Kuhn's sentence, he was deported back to Germany. With the fall of the Bund's top leadership and America coming closer to its entry into World War II, the organization's membership shrank, and insufficient funds could not cover the day-to-day operations of Camp Siegfried. On June 26, 1941, Camp Siegfried defaulted on a $12,000 mortgage that was held by A.V. Development Corporation.[12]

The final blow to the Long Island Bund came when the FBI arrested seventy-two mid-level management members on charges of conspiracy to obstruct selective service and alien registration. While conducting the raid, the FBI seized propaganda, Nazi newspapers, radios, cameras, firearms and ammunition, which were distributed throughout Nassau and Suffolk Counties.[13] The headlines about the raid and the excessive weapons further isolated active Bund members, as locals no longer perceived them as harmless but as a domestic militarized threat. Within defense contracting on Long Island, all open Bund supporters and members were fired on the grounds of being security threats. With all the efforts of law enforcement and proposed plea deals of indicted Bund leadership, the membership and Nazi loyalists' rolls were not disclosed and remain a mystery. Despite the dismantling of the Bund and the breaking up the spy rings, the Nazi threat evolved. If the Nazis could not infiltrate the population to support their cause, they would attempt export sabotage and fear into New Yorkers' and Long Islanders' everyday lives.

2

FBI DETAINEES AND COUNTERINTELLIGENCE

Within the same week that America entered the war, the FBI expanded its investigations of German and Japanese businesses throughout America. In New York City, hundreds of German and Japanese banks, shipping firms and other companies were forced to close, and their assets were frozen. In total, throughout the country, $5 million to $7 million worth of property was frozen and seized. Hundreds of businessmen with deep connections to these firms were arrested and sent to Camp Upton's alien internment camps. The people placed in these camps were potentially dangerous to the war effort and were to stay in the camp until it was deemed that they were not a risk to the war effort. In total, fifty-one Germans, eleven Italians and eighty-six Japanese-born New York residents were sent to Upton's internment camp until the war's end. The estimated two thousand Japanese citizens in the New York City area were put under a curfew that applied to only them until it was determined they were not a threat by the federal government.[14]

In Nassau County, the FBI conducted roundups of German nationalists who were potential intelligence threats. The roundup brought in three suspects: Lisette Kapri, who was residing in Roosevelt Field Hotel with falsified paperwork that stated she was from Russia; Rolf Quarck, a German nationalist from Port Washington; and Ernest Nolte, a known German chemist who was working as an upholster in Garden City.[15] In Suffolk County, local law enforcement officials arrested Bruno Johannes Valianski of Central Islip under suspicion of Nazi collaboration and robbery. Valianski, a self-proclaimed Gestapo agent, was a recruiter for the local German American Cannon Fodder Armies of the Third Reich.[16] This group was a militarized Nazi group with the goal of assisting the German cause in America.

After the roundup of suspects and break up of Nazi militaristic groups throughout Long Island, America's entry into the war and the prior discovery of Nazi spy rings across Long Island, the FBI became more creative in breaking up spy rings and collecting counterintelligence. In the weeks after America declared war on Japan and Germany, the FBI discovered a series of spy rings that led to Nazi spies defecting in a panic. Communication delays between spies and their handlers gave the FBI an advantage in creating counterintelligence agents and even double agents. A defector, Jorge Mosquera, was a Nazi spy who defected to American agents in Uruguay. Mosquera was provided with funds to establish a shortwave radio station on Long Island for him to transmit information from other contacts in the New York City area.[17]

Working with Mosquera, the FBI found two properties that were used as safehouses. The first house in Wading River, which was referred to as the Benson House, was almost hidden in a dense pine forest. This property was a radio transmission site. The second safehouse, an office rented in New York City at 1475 Broadway Avenue, Room 1210, was utilized as a secret drop-off point for German agents which operated as an Uruguayan businessman's office. The information picked up from the Broadway Avenue location was dropped off at the Benson House for transmission. Agent Donworth Johnson had his family move into the house while he posed as a person suffering from tuberculosis. The FBI established a shortwave radio station at the house to broadcast counterintelligence to one of the Nazi defector's handlers in Hamburg Germany. The dense brush that surrounded the house was perfect for hiding the antennae of the shortwave radio. To avoid attention from the excessive use of electricity, the agents used a generator to power the radio equipment.

With the Nazi safehouse identified and the Benson House being used as a false safehouse, the FBI's chain of contacts became the only priority for the organization to maintain. Mosquera's contacts included Elmer Carlton, the owner of the Remle-Carlton Shipping Company, which was used by the local German Bund to ship and receive goods from Nazi Germany and would have been embargoed due to the escalation of the war and its ties to Nazi Germany. This contact was essential because it directly linked German Bund leader, Fritz Kuhn, and local Bund leaders to Nazi Germany and to Hjalmar Schacht, Hitler's finance minster.[18] Unfortunately, early into the counteroperation, Carlton got suspicious of his daily meetings with Mosquera and started to distance himself from domestic spy operations. Hans Blum, another contact Mosquera had carried over with him, was a German army officer who attended espionage school in Hamburg. His key role in the Nazi ring was to establish a chain of spies while operating a chemical shipping business called Remy and Company. Blum became a vital unsuspected resource in achieving the FBI's goals. The FBI operation at Benson House fed Germans false information on the number of troops being shipped to Europe, and it got information that Germany was trying to obtain an atomic bomb.[19]

The misinformation from the Benson House radio transmissions fed German agents intel that influenced the success of the allies' D-Day invasion and America's decision to develop an atomic bomb. The most disturbing information gathered was on how far entrenched the Nazi spy ring had become in New York City and Long Island. Nazi spy applicants were sent to training programs that were managed by the Gestapo, and once they graduated, they were planted across New York City and Long Island. The earliest traceable plant dated as far back as 1936. Even with all the warnings of the rise of German nationalist organizations, officials only started paying attention after vital military technological secrets were leaked.

As the FBI gathered intel, a twenty-year-old army private, Karl Max Wacker, was busted for spying within the armed service. Wacker was busted at the Camp Upton base hospital after suffering injuries he had received in combat during the army's Berlin campaign. Army generals were in disbelief, as he had not only hidden in plain sight, but he had had a distinguished career in the army. His loyalties shifted toward the Germans when his parents were picked up by the FBI for being suspected dangerous aliens. Wacker then enrolled in a Nazi spy school and told the people closest to him that he would "do anything he could to help the Germans win the war."[20] The information he may have leaked to his German handlers in Berlin included the location of airplane manufacturing plants across Long Island and troop convoy movements. Suspicion of Wacker arose after he disappeared for a month prior to a battle in the European theater; Wacker's cover story was he had been captured by Germans during the confusion of a fire fight and escaped to the advancing Soviet troops.[21] When cross-examined by federal agents in Upton, Wacker claimed he was suffering from amnesia due to a wound he had received in combat.

Following the bust of private Wacker, the army faced another devastating leak from a Nazi spy within military ranks. In December 1945, Sergeant

Frank Hart of the United States Army was arrested for conspiring to commit wartime espionage. Frank Hart, a second-generation German, split his residency between Berlin, Germany, and Arizona Avenue in North Babylon. While he was in Germany a decade prior to the start of the war, Hart enlisted in the Hitler-Jugend, or Nazi Youth, movement and moved through the ranks to join the Reinsfueheer's Storm Troopers. After coming home to North Babylon in 1941, Hart had a great deal of money, which he told his neighbors had come from well-to-do grandparents.[22] Similar to dozens of others in North Babylon, Hart enlisted in the army following the Japanese attacks on Pearl Harbor. While enlisted in the army, Hart became interested in aircraft mechanics and pursued a position in the field. Once he obtained the position, the Nazis assigned him to document American military plane technology and weaponry for Nazi agents in South America and Europe. The resulting damage or severity of his leaked information was never known. What made these busts so devastating was not the knowledge that intelligence had been leaked but that Germany had the ability to infiltrate the American army even while it was on high guard.

3.

CIVILIAN DEFENSE

On the eve of December 7, 1941, Long Island became an active domestic front against a foreign threat. Long Island prior to 1941 was divided on America's entry into the war. A segment of the population bought into the Nazi rhetoric, but closer to 1941, public opinion shifted, and the Nazis became viewed as a threat. The Nazis were perceived as threats after newsreels and newspaper headlines began reporting on unsuspected Nazi invasions of countries that were previously thought to have been at peace with Germany.

On December 9, 1941, at 12:35 a.m., an air raid whistle sounded throughout Nassau County. Following the air raid whistle, residents were in a state of hysteria and panic over a potential aerial bombing. The following day, the headlines of all the local papers confirmed the fears of locals: "Hostile Planes off Long Island Reported: Mitchel Field Fliers Out." This was not the first time enemy bombers had flown over Long Island. In January 1941, four unidentified bombers had flown over the Long Island Sound, and the Mitchel Field Fliers were sent out. The only difference between this event and the event of December 9 was that America was officially at war in December, and the horrors of Pearl Harbor were still fresh in locals' minds. Following these events Long Island went on the defensive. The following week, on Monday, December 15, 1941, a detachment of military police from Camp Upton moved into Roosevelt Field.[23] The establishment of twenty-four-hour air patrols were ordered out of Mitchel Field, and twelve aircraft observation posts were established. These local events and the national news of the attack on Pearl Harbor created the sense of urgency Long Island needed to unify behind a war effort.

The military was welcomed into local communities, and members of the military were embraced as heroes. Civilian and military partnerships were formed where air corps surveillance was lacking. With the lack of spotters, Brigadier General Glenn O. Barcus, who commanded the First Fighter Command, telegrammed North Hempstead's director of servicemen, Harold Ray, to organize plane spotting sites.[24] Within Nassau County, airplane spotter sites were organized in the communities of Freeport, Great Neck, Hicksville, Inwood, Manhasset, North Bellmore, Oyster Bay, Port Washington, Roslyn, Sea Cliff, Valley Stream, Mineola and Wheatly Hills. One of the tallest buildings, the First National Bank Building on Sunrise Highway in Freeport, had a state-of-the-art aircraft spotting and warning station assembled by early 1942. Over two thousand volunteer spotters were assembled and trained.

In early 1942, Suffolk County started assembling spotters. Since Suffolk County was less densely populated, the number of spotters needed there was significantly smaller. The Islip Town aircraft observation posts were commissioned at the Central Islip Hospital Administration Building, Islip High School, Sayville High School, the Brentwood Public School Building and the Bohemia Public School Building. These buildings were chosen because of their heights and their positions on higher ground. The observation posts were assigned 190 men and women who were certified observers. The observers' shifts were three hours long during the day and two hours long at night; each shift was covered by teams of two. To maintain a flow of new certified volunteers and to keep current observers up to date with enemy aircraft, an evening certification and recertification course was given weekly at the Brentwood and Islip Public Schools. The observers remained active throughout most of the war, but in May 29, 1944, the group was disbanded by the military.

Despite the overwhelming number of volunteer civilian airplane spotters, Suffolk County still had a gap in protection. The construction of an air base in Montauk was sluggishly taking shape in 1940. With the Japanese bombing of Pearl Harbor and the anxiety of enemy planes potentially attacking Long Island and New York City landmarks, construction was accelerated and completed by early 1942. The base, Camp Hero, was named after General Andrew Hero, who had recently died prior to completion of the base. The base, located close to the Montauk Point, was equipped with a series of sixteen-inch antiaircraft guns in concrete bunkers facing the ocean. The aircraft spotters were stationed at their posts twenty-four hours a day. The base, at the peak of World War II, had 640 soldiers and officers stationed on 750 acres. The base was disguised as a fishing village in an effort to fool enemy planes. Fortunately, the bunker guns were never fired outside of annual tests or drills. Later, toward the end of the war, the base constructed a radar station, which became the largest on Long Island.

Following the construction of Camp Hero at Montauk Point in 1943, another air base was constructed in West Hampton. This base was designed to be an eastern extension of Mitchel Field in Hempstead. This new air base was meant to be able to send over a thousand fighter planes into combat, but the most distinctive features put in the base's original plans were its underground bunkers and an airplane hangar. Added to the plans was an underground hangar that was bomb proof and designed to withstand any German attack; this was built as an effort to keep fighter planes undamaged and ready to take off following an attack. The construction of the bunkers was a direct response to the fears generated by German fighter planes leveling London during their many bombing raids.

Further expanding access to the air corps' space, the newly constructed West Hampton base was connected to the area's few private air strips, which were acquired by the military. This base became home to 437th Army Air Corps Unit. This command flew antisubmarine patrols throughout the New York City area. While the construction of Camp Hero and the eastern air base, Mitchel Field's flier patrols in Hempstead and trained civilian aircraft spotters were successful in reducing locals' fears of an air strike, they were not fool proof in preventing an attack. A defense force had to be formed in case there was a strike. Communities across New York had to have preventive measures to reduce potential causalities and keep order in the event of an air strike. Planning for what many people viewed as the inevitable local culture shifted aggressively toward vigilance.

New additional safety measures were taken to protect the home front; local officials had a goal to train four thousand air raid wardens throughout all the counties in Long Island.[25] The air raid wardens had a wide range of duties. The job description included enforcing blackout drills and managing the emergency needs if there was an air raid. This position was created through the Office for Emergency Management (OEM) in May 1941. The main goals of this new civilian defense program were to not only provide protection for the civilian population but to build a bridge between the military and civilians. This partnership got full participation in war programs and military joint efforts. State aid was added to any federal grant allocated

Above: Sixteen-inch antiaircraft guns were built into a concrete bunker at Camp Hero Montauk. *Courtesy of the Montauk Historical Society.*

Left: A Camp Hero Radar Station installed toward the end of World War II. *Courtesy of Christopher Verga.*

to this partnership due to New York State governor Herbert Lehman's appointment to the State Council of Defense seven months earlier.

The State Council of Defense had three divisions: the Division of Civilian Mobilization (prior to 1942, this was referred to as Division of Volunteer Participation), the Division of Civilian Protection and the Division of Industry and Labor. The most innovative idea that came out of this legislation and council was the Block Plan. The Block Plan organized community war effort programs, such as salvage metal, transportation and carpools and war savings.[26] Emergency healthcare was added to the Civilian Defense Council's goals under the Division of Civilian Protection following the Bolton Act of 1943. The Bolton Act granted future U.S. Public Health Service employees all-expenses-paid scholarships to nursing schools, but they had to enroll under the U.S. Cadet Nursing Corps after graduation. The nurse cadets were assigned to military operations or essential civilian nursing stations until the end of the war.[27] The nurse corps would, later in the war, serve in the locally established prisoner of war camps by providing vital health care to recently captured enemy soldiers.

With the introduction of state laws, a structured model and allocated money in place prior to the federal grants, the mobilization of a civilian defense force came quicker in New York than it did in other states. President Franklin Roosevelt took notice of New York City and the surrounding suburbs' successful mobilization and appointed New York City mayor Firoello La Guardia to head the Office of Civilian Defense. Once he was on the job, La Guardia stressed the importance of recruiting volunteers by stating:

> Don't let the good news from Italy lull you into a false sense of security. If Hitler or Hirohito feel that bombing New York City is worth the price, they will pay it. But—your city is prepared for such an attack and is ready to meet the needs of men, women and children who may be affected by it.…America learned the hard way that war can happen here. Your city is prepared. Are you?[28]

Throughout the New York City and Long Island areas, Civilian Defense Volunteer Offices (CDVO) were opened to draw in as many volunteers as possible. Nassau County civil defense commander Sherman Moreland opened eight volunteer offices across the county along the south shore. Open-house training sessions in emergency situations through the use of incendiary bombs and war gases were set up in Hewitt Schools.[29] Advertisements were taken out in local papers to encourage women to join the civil defense efforts. Nightly drills of blackouts five to ten miles from the shoreline were done every day; blackouts were meant to confuse any enemy of where the shore started and ended.

On September 15, 1941, one of the first air raid drills was conducted in Port Washington, with 1,500 residents set to test their readiness in the case of an emergency. The drill exposed the weaknesses of the community, and if it had been a real air raid, one hundred locals would have been killed. At first, many residents disregarded the failed test, but after December 7, 1941, the failures of the September test were revisited. Examination of the failures and gaps in civilian defense created a community outpour of support and a demand for more training programs on community safety and more air raid wardens. A federal and state goal was modified to have one air raid warden for every 125 people, which created a need for 650 more wardens in Nassau County.[30] The duties of the warden's office were expanded from organizing blackouts to commanding a fire warden, an auxiliary police force, emergency food management, a chaplain and utility repair.

Following the reorganization and expansion of civilian volunteer groups, the first large-scale drill occurred on March 25, 1942. The blackout drill expanded throughout the entire 331 square miles of Nassau County, with all 125,000 residential houses and 420,000 residents participating.[31] This drill, unlike the prior small-scale drills, was carried out almost flawlessly. In Rockville Center, air defense drills became more creative when simulating emergency events. This event was not a blackout test but an emergency response event. The practice event simulated a three-hundred-pound bomb going off and trapping people in the debris of sixty buildings. The fire department, medical team and chemical agent team were tested on response time, followed by the evacuation time of residents. The community air raid wardens, using Rockville Center's example, simulated disaster drills in the villages of Hempstead and Lynbrook monthly. After a while, these air raid and disaster drills became the new normal in Nassau, most of Suffolk, Queens and Brooklyn. By mid-1942 one in every four Nassau County residents were members of a branch of the civilian defense.[32] This number was a success that other areas struggled to replicate. Unlike most counties in New York, Nassau had a growing population, but it still managed to keep new residents engaged, which further grew the number of active members in its civilian defense corps.

Suffolk County, unlike Nassau, had fewer resources available for an organized civilian defense corps. The majority of the county was made up

This page: Civilian Defense volunteers in a training course on how to use a switchboard. Air Raid Warden Programs were held in every town, but the large expos, like the one in the picture, took place in Madison Square Garden. *Courtesy of the Library of Congress Image Collection.*

of the old estates of the richest families in America and large-scale farms. Some towns, such as Bay Shore, maintained an industrial-based economy, which provided them with the opportunity to have organized civilian defense operations. The civilian corps' central focus was not the protection of densely populated areas but of the county's transportation hubs. Across Suffolk, limited highways and train tracks traversed only a small number of towns, which created a demand for a civilian motor corps. The first community to set up a successful motor corps was Bay Shore. The motor corps provided transportation between military bases, to hospitals, war-based manufacturing hubs and the homes of needed doctors.

Bay Shore's motor corps, which was originally trained for civilian evacuation in times of an air raid, transported doctors from Southside Hospitals to General Mason Hospital in Brentwood and Camp Upton. Other routes utilized by the motor corps in times of medical emergencies ran between the docks in Bay Shore and the coast guard base on Fire Island. The motor corps, once at the docks, would wait for the ferry to drop off a patient or supplies. When the bay was frozen, the motor corps would drive across the ice to deliver doctors and supplies to the Fire Island Coast Guard Base. At times, this was the only option to get supplies to the bases on the barrier islands, as boats were not able to cut through and reach the state channels.

Other civilian defense outfits in Bay Shore included the canteen corps. This group shared needed resources with the military bases and served as

Civilian Motor Corps of Bay Shore. The Bay Shore Civilian Corps transported supplies and sailors from the Bay Shore docks to Mason General Hospital in Brentwood. *Courtesy of the Bay Shore Historical Society.*

a welcoming committee for troops stationed within the county. This corps serviced Camp Upton and General Mason Hospital, which kept blood banks stocked and coal abundant throughout the winter months. The welcoming role of the corps included providing sandwiches and coffee to all of Camp Upton's incoming and departing soldiers at Patchogue Train Station.

The greatest goal of the civilian defense was to create a citizenry that was vigilant of a threat. The air raid drills shifted the pro-German sentiment of the area to one of unification against a shared threat. The threat identified daily in the drills made German espionage harder due to local suspicion of who may have been a spy working for Hitler. This unification also created a morale boost for soldiers who were going off to combat. Having all Americans unified against a common enemy and aligned with a shared vision for victory kept production flowing and volunteers joining all of the military branches despite reports of causalities.

4

MOBILIZATION OF TROOPS

Throughout the United States, 16 million people were mobilized in the military branches. Out of that 16 million, a little under 1 million were from New York, and 10 million had been drafted into service. For New York to have had that many veterans from World War II, and with over half of all people serving nationally to have been drafted the local selective service and draft boards had to have been essential.

The mobilization of the military was in line with public opinion. In 1939, the majority of Americans did not want to get involved with the war but supported selling supplies to England. According to a study on American public opinion and World War II from the political science department of the Massachusetts Institute of Technology, support in 1940 had shifted, with 67 percent of Americans saying that it should be a priority to help England by any means necessary and 33 percent saying it was important for Americans to stay natural or out of the war completely.

The Selective Training and Service Act of 1940 functioned locally through Selective Service Boards, which managed records and personal files of people within the assigned district. The other objectives of these locally managed boards were to oversee the registration of any male over the age of eighteen for selective service. The majority of the estimated 1 million New Yorkers who served in the military during World War II would have had their first stop at the local draft board. The Hempstead Draft Board became the most active one in the county. In December 1940, the Hempstead Board set a quota of 480 men from January to June 30, 1941.

To better reach the quota, the board set individual quotas for the largest Nassau County towns. For the month of January alone, the Nassau town of Glen Cove had 13 men sign up for the draft, Hicksville had 14, Great Neck had 12, Port Washington had 10, Westbury had 16, Bellmore had 12, Freeport had 13, Baldwin had 8, Hempstead had 16, Long Beach had 11, Rockville Centre had 11, Valley Stream had 11, Franklin Square had 14 and Floral Park had 9. All Black draftees were deferred until February, or until the Black draft units were organized.

December 7, 1941, marked a dramatic change in military recruitment. The ethnic group with the most men who signed up for military service were the Italians. Decades of biases surrounding Italian immigration were due to a labor glut and stereotypes of the small percentage of the group's involvement in organized crime. Local differences among those who practiced Protestantism and the Italians who practiced Catholicism created a backlash of Klan resurgence. Klan members lobbied for anti-Italian immigration legislation on a federal level, and locally, Klan members lobbied to block the construction of any Catholic church. Despite all the state and local biases and anti-immigration restrictions, Italians were still on track to become the largest ethnic group on Long Island by 1940.

Originally, the Italians migrated to Long Island in the early twentieth century and comprised 30 percent of the area's day and farm labors. Within two decades, Italians began to make up 22 percent of the grocery store business owners and operators in downtown hubs across Long Island. Throughout Long Island, this rise in Italian business ownership played out in the form of even more aggressive anti-immigrant feelings, with claims that Italians were not capable of being American. Local banks attempted to block funding for Italian business startups, but the Italian community became self-funded; Italians pooled their money together and invested in each other.

With the outbreak of World War II, new biases emerged on federal level. As the population of Italians grew to make up an estimated 25 percent of Long Island's population, federal and state governments debated if they would be a threat; some even called for all Italians to be classified as alien enemies due to the rise of fascism in their home country. However, America's need for soldiers was fulfilled by the 750,000 to 1.5 million Italians who signed up for service across the nation. It was as if Italian Americans were attempting to show their willingness to make a sacrifice for an American cause and prove the bigots wrong.

One person who signed up for service despite bigotry he encountered was Angelo Termini. Originally from Queens, Angelo came to America from

Italy at the age of nine. Before settling in Glen Cove, Angelo was bullied for his language and accent, but when war broke out, he became battlefield tested. While in the army, he fought in Sicily and France in the Normandy Invasion, which earned him the Purple Heart, Silver Star and Bronze Star. Termini's bravery was only surpassed by the fourteen Italians who awarded the Congressional Medal of Honor for their brave conduct on the battlefield.

Impressed by the mobilization of New York Italians, and in confronting his own bias, United States attorney general Francis Biddle attended a Columbus Day celebration at Carnegie Hall to discuss the American government's gratitude for Italian Americans. During his speech, Biddle stated:

> *When war broke out, we declared the Italians alien enemies, and time would tell the story of their loyalties. Experience has borne me out. You have met the test. Your loyalty to democracy, which has given you this chance, which you proved well, proves you're trustworthy. Your love of freedom gives all that is in you for this nation, which you are now fighting to preserve. Thus, it will never be said that Italians are a disloyal group.*[33]

The Italians' display of loyalty to America became a part of their identity, and they carved out a piece of ownership in American society. This wave of Italian patriotism and their display of loyalty to America was reflected in all the downtown businesses that were run by them. There, Italian Americans displayed pictures of loved ones in military uniforms, draped in stars-and-stripes banners. These displays reflected the community's praise of local high-ranking veterans with extravagant ceremonies and parades organized by local Italian Catholic groups and other community organizations in downtown hubs.

General George C. Marshall, who had been a seasonal resident of Ocean Beach since 1930, had a ceremony that made him an honorary citizen, which was publicized throughout Long Island. Marshall drew attention when he arrived in the area by landing an army amphibian plane in the bay; his landing was followed by a crew on large rowboats, which met him and brought him to shore. His home, similar to his landing, drew a lot of attention. Marshall's Ocean Beach house was retrofitted with trap doors and secret passages by the army to protect him from any attempts on his life. During the war, Marshall would spend his time relaxing and planning in his home, but his presence was used for mobilization drives to recruit volunteers for the armed service. Out of a population of eighty-one residents, thirty-three signed up for military service, and an additional thirty-four signed up for a civilian volunteer service. This was one of the highest percentages of a population signing up for war effort in Long Island.

In Smithtown, there may have been no General Marshall visits or any large Italian populations proclaiming their support, but there was no shortage on war support. Similar to other western Suffolk towns, Smithtown's economy was localized in fishing, farming and small-scale manufacturing. With America's entry into World War II, the lure of leaving small-town America became an option for many young residents. Feeding into their desire to explore the world outside of Smithtown was the sense of patriotic duty. Longtime resident and World War II veteran James Gouras of Smithtown said that, back then, the downtown area was covered in posters that promoted military service, stars-and-stripes banners hung from all stores, pictures of recently deployed soldiers were

First-generation Italian Americans signed up for the service in large numbers. Hubert Verga of Elmont (the author's grandfather) enlisted in the United States Army. *Courtesy of Christopher Verga.*

displayed in store windows and almost everyone he knew had signed up for the service in some form. During Gouras's senior year of high school, a recruiter went to his school to talk to his class about the need to serve, which resulted in twelve people signing up. The twelve, including himself, were to report to basic training following their high school graduation.

Thirty minutes west of Smithtown, George Allison of Syosset watched his father maintain a country estate and was the next in line to assume the same job. Despite the potential job stability, George had a strong desire to use the war as an excuse to explore the world outside of the country estate. Allison's mom was concerned about the potential danger he could encounter if he signed up for the navy, so he eased his mother's concerns by signing up for the United States Coast Guard. Allision explained to his mother the expectations of his service were in the title of the branch—he was going to be guarding the coast. But Allison and his mother did not know that he would be shipped to serve in the Battle of Okinawa, where he was awarded four Bronze Stars.

This sudden surge of young people signing up for the military was not portrayed as the young taking advantage of new opportunities; it was portrayed as the young carrying out an act of patriotism and self-sacrifice. This portrayal of martyrdom highlighted in local papers throughout Long Island further fanned the flames of encouragement for young people and unified everyone behind a shared common enemy. Karl Heiman of East Meadow embraced the shared common enemy and had personal experience that pointed to the urgency to purge Europe of fascism. Heiman had migrated to America from Germany two weeks before World War II broke out. When he attempted to sign up, he was denied due to the region his family was from and the fact that he was not a citizen (citizenship was a factor in being accepted into the armed service at the time). When Pearl Harbor was bombed, he attempted to sign up for the army again, pleading with the recruiter that "he [knew] firsthand on the dangers of Hitler" and that Hitler had twenty-two members of his family locked up (these twenty-two family members later died in concentration camps). Soon after being rejected, Heiman was drafted into the army, despite the restrictions that held him back from volunteering.

Entire families signed up for the service and were praised as local heroes. Similar to Heiman, Paul Butkereit of East Rockway was a first-generation German immigrant. Butkereit was a naturalized citizen and the only son of the Butkereit family; he was encouraged to sign up due to the fact that his father narrowly escaped Germany during the turmoil that followed World War I. Paul signed up for the U.S. Army Air Corps following the bombing of Pearl Harbor. Josephine Verga of Cedarhurst had all six of her sons sign up for the army and air force. They were all shipped overseas to European and Asian campaigns as either tail gunners in B-24 bombers, quarter masters or grounded crew for the air force. In Suffolk County Islip, Claude Truax had five of his six sons sign up for the service. Four went into the army and air corps, and one served in the civilian defense corps. Truax's sixth son, who did not sign up, was handicapped. All of his enlisted sons collectively earned four bronze stars.

Having all of a family's sons sign up for active military duty was a direct violation of the Sole Survivor Policy. This policy, which was ignored by many families, was to prevent a family from losing an entire generation to combat deaths. The law stated that not all brothers within the same family can serve in combat. In Bethpage, three brothers, Charles, Joseph and Henry Butehorn, signed up for the army, and all three were deployed. Charles signed up for the army in June 1943, despite getting a scholarship to study at Syracuse University; he was killed in action in France the following year. His other brother Joseph was killed in the Pacific soon after, in 1945.

This page: William Benish of Nassau County, wanting to do serve his country, enlisted in the U.S. Army Air Corps. William Benish is pictured here in Mitchel Field. *Courtesy of Frank Benish.*

The last brother, Henry, who was stationed southern Italy, was sent home under a directive of the defense department in an effort to comply with the Solo Survivor Policy.

While enrollment was on an upswing, local schools began to focus on how to prepare their graduating senior classes to meet the needs of the war. In 1942, New York State governor Lehman mandated an obstacle course lesson to be added to the gym curriculum of every high school. In a press statement, Lehman stated, "Not only should we send our young men into the army in excellent physical shape, but [we] must also condition them to do strenuous factory tasks—and that includes women, too." In addition to the wartime changes to gym class, Lehman started an army drill camp program to get young men ready for basic training following high school. This program included rifle training, which was instructed by members of the American Legion. In an effort to not exclude female students from military training, female students got the basic rifle training but were encouraged to join the motor corps instead of female units in the military.

By the end of 1942, twenty-six Nassau High Schools had rolled out a basic training preparation program for their senior classes. These programs followed by army-installed pre-entry programs, pending the students' completion of high school, which increased military enrollment. The first wave of troop mobilization included men younger than twenty-six, with no children. These high school programs allowed local towns to exceed their quotas without a problem.

Closer to 1945, the demand for enlisted men was once again a high priority. Soldiers were needed for an occupying force in Europe, and there was a potential need for soldiers to conduct an invasion of Japan; all of this would require at least one million more troops. Soldiers older than twenty-six had families and professions. To free up the older age groups who were hesitant to enlist or eager for deferments, Congress passed the Recruitment Act. This act extended benefits to the family dependents of military members. The allowance amount prior to the act was $37.50 a month, but under this act, a wife and one child received $80.00 a month; this would equal out to around $20.00 extra for each dependent.[34] In another attempt to spur demand and maintain enlisted soldiers, a new sign-on bonus of $50 was passed, and servicemembers were given the ability to suggest where they would like to serve. Servicemembers could choose to serve in Alaska, the European theater, Africa and the Middle East, the Pacific theater, the Mid-Pacific, China or the Caribbean. The choice to pick a location was not guaranteed, and soldiers' demands were not always priority. These options, however, increased the number of men enlisting, which forced the military to open five more recruitment stations in the towns of Hempstead, Lynbrook, Glen Cove, Huntington and Riverhead. These recruitment stations took the lead in acquiring new soldiers, as they had higher recruitment numbers than the old selective service and draft boards.

With all the media blitz concentrated on the need to serve and the popularity of being a man in uniform, little over 30 percent of Americans in 1940 wanted the nation to remain neutral. An even larger number of Americans were against any conscription order or draft into military service. In a *Newsday* editorial in 1941, conscription was criticized as "a step to draw Americans into an aggressive war to enlarge the profits of Wall Street."[35] But after the attacks on Pearl Harbor, the number of advocates for neutrality and people who opposed the draft started to shrink, but they remained a vocal outlier.

On March 21, 1944, the voices of pro-neutral draftees became public in the form of a draft board investigation. The Long Beach Draft Board 720 came to the attention of General Ames Brown, who was the New York State director of selective service. The draft office was giving out a large amount of 4-F cases, which were hardship exemptions from military service and various other deferments. The numbers of these deferments were cited as "being unusually large in proportion to the population." Following an investigation, John Jacobs, the chief clerk of the draft board, was arrested by federal agents. Jacobs was alleged to have taken two bottles of whisky worth seventy-five dollars, two turkeys and a steak for granting deferments.[36] His arrest followed the arrest Theophrasios Delynnis, a restaurant owner in Rockville Center who was charged with bribing Jacobs.

Another arrest related to the Long Beach Draft Board scandal was that of Robert O'Grady of Brooklyn, who used to work at the Long Beach Draft Board before he was transferred to a Brooklyn draft board. While in Brooklyn, O'Grady sold deferments for $250 each. While building a case, the FBI made a deal with the cochairman of the Long Beach Draft Board Herman Wood and Herman Duckman, a Hofstra student who attempted to get a deferment. Duckman was classified as 2-A, which made him eligible to not be drafted into army, but it allowed him to join the merchant marines. Both men were called in to testify against Jacobs and O'Grady. Woods publically changed his testimony and told the media there were "no irregularities [he] witnessed."

During the trial, Theophrasios Delynnis was convicted of illegally possessing a draft classification card and was sentenced to six years in

Left: An advertisement for men to enlist before being drafted and participate in local military drill preparations. The advertisement was funded by the Hempstead American Legion Post 390. *Courtesy of the Hofstra University Library Special Collection.*

Below: Recently drafted men finished boot camp at Camp Upton and headed to Patchogue for leave time. *Courtesy of the Longwood Library, Bayles Local History Room and Photograph Archives.*

prison and a $1,000 fine. For lesser time, Delynnis testified against Jacobs and O'Grady, but with the changing testimony of Woods, both Jacobs and O'Grady were acquitted. Following the war, Delynnis was part of a bigger group of draft dodgers who received a presidential pardon. But a pardon from the president did not mean Delynnis's community forgot about the negative media attention he had received. In 1946, due to the public attention, local veterans boycotted his restaurant, and in a final blow, the Village of Rockville Centre refused the renewal of his restaurant license. The village council argued its refusal was on grounds that he had been convicted of a felony. In an effort to appeal the ruling, Delynnis argued that the business was owned in his wife's name, but the board held firm to its ruling.

The ramifications of the Long Beach Draft Board scandal included a political shift in the city politics. Democratic mayor Theodore Ornstein and his administration were all investigated for possible involvement in selling deferments. This investigation was due to the mayor's appointment of the draft board members. The administration and mayor were quickly cleared of any wrongdoing, but the mayor and his administration were voted out due to veterans' groups pulling support away from him.

Other forms of resistance to the draft included some individuals' full change in identity. Vernon Duval of Port Washington was drafted in late December 1941 at the Port Washington Draft Board. After being drafted, Vernon quickly moved to New York City and abandoned his wife and kids. While in New York City, Vernon assumed the last name of Kelly and registered as a forty-five-year-old, making him too old to be drafted for service. Vernon got a job as a bartender, remarried without divorcing his first wife and started a new family. While evading the draft, Vernon had a warrant issued for his arrest. Four years later, while stopping over in Bay Shore, locals recognized Vernon, as he had been in the area visiting family. When he was arrested, Vernon was charged with evading the draft, and the lesser charge of bigamy was dropped. Duval was held on $5,000 bail and pled guilty.

Conflicts with selective service boards were not just confined to pro- and antiwar sentiment and selling deferments. The reclassification of draft status was tied into keeping wartime employees compliant. The demand in wartime manufacturing created an economic boom like Long Island had never seen, and the need for a skilled workforce emerged within the limited population. To keep skilled workers from being drafted and shipped overseas, employers advocated for the draft boards to reclassify these workers as class II-B. This classification shielded skilled workers from military service, as they were considered essential military contractors. People who had resigned from military-based contracting had sixty days to find a job in a related military contracting field to keep the classification. Failure to find another job in the required field resulted in a reclassification for active duty.

In Freeport, Columbian Bronze Corp, was contracted to make propellers for the navy but ran into conflict with its workforce. Workers started walking off the job and striking over workplace conditions that included being unprotected from heavy dust and airborne fibers that were causing them to have sore throats and other breathing problems. The workers also demanded water fountains and proper bathrooms. In an effort to break the strike, the Freeport Selective Service Board reclassified all of the workers as class I-A, making them all eligible to be drafted into military service. This reclassification of the striking workers brought to light the fragmented interpretation of what qualifies workers for deferment. After an examination of all the Nassau County draft boards, Freeport was found to be the only board that was drafting men over the age of twenty-six who had previously been classified as essential wartime workers. The reclassification of the striking workers and the statics of classifying wartime contractors as eligible for military service promoted an investigation by New York selective service director Ames T. Brown. The conclusion of his investigation was that Freeport's numbers were due to a misinterpretation of the guidelines on behalf of factory managers and draft board workers.

At the close of 1945, Selective Service Appeal Board 14, which serviced Nassau and Suffolk Counties, had twenty-one thousand deferments through appeals. The overall majority of the deferments were for farm laborers and essential defense contract workers. Board members Charles Dimon and Raymond Fish granted farm deferments, which were class 2-C and class 3-C. Dimon and Fish granted deferments for county farmers and farm labors at a high rate. When questioned about these deferments, chairperson Ferdinand Haber defended Dimon and Fish, stating, "These critics are lacking in a true understanding of conflicting demands of the fighting front, the production of food and the food front. But consequently, the many young men who entered the defense plant workforce became valuable to their employers and get deferments as well."[37]

The rate at which these farm deferments were granted was high, not just in Long Island, but across the country. Throughout the war over 300,000 agricultural labor deferments were granted, and southern senators referred to farms, especially in the North, as "havens for draft dodgers."

In Hicksville, a total of 326 2-C and 3-C classifications were granted in three years, which stood out due to the estimated 3,000-person population of the town. Inspectors under the command of county agricultural agent Howard Campbell had all the farms whose addresses been provided for the deferments inspected to see if they were producing the food output that was needed for the war effort. All three hundred farmers and farm labors were cleared and met the quota, but they were monitored. If the farm's output went below the quota, the workers could be reclassified for military service. Despite efforts from Washington, D.C., pressure from local officials to close the loopholes for farmers and public outcry over fears of a low food supply, which were fueled by headlines of limited food supplies and starvation across Europe and Asia, none of the proposed laws against the farmers ever became ratified. Further blocking any farmer draft laws was the rationing of food in America; this gave the appearance of food scarcity, which provided the farmers a counterargument against sending them and their laborers into active service.

While draftees and enlistees flooded into the various branches of the military, the then-current Long Island bases were starting to be redesigned in an effort to reflect the demand. Mitchel Field, prior to becoming an established military base, was a landing strip for hobbyist aviators. In 1917, following the end of World War I, the field became a training ground for American aviators in combat. The base was later named in honor of John Purroy Mitchel, who was the New York City mayor who enlisted in the service and was killed in training. On the eve of World War II, the base was reorganized as an air defense post. The base became a priority due to its proximity to New York City and other air defense manufacturing plants.

In early 1943, Mitchel Field formed the First Air Force Command. Mitchel Field was one of a few bases responsible for guarding the region between the Northeast and the Great Lakes. The United States Air Force Command was not the same as the modern-day United States Air Force. Mitchel Field was still under the command of the United States Army Air Corps. The establishment of the United States Air Force came after the war in 1947. During the war, Mitchel Field trained some of America's bravest pilots. The troops there were trained on how to operate B-24 Liberator, P-47 Thunderbolt, P-63 Airacobra, DC-3 Curtis and C-46 commando troop and equipment transport planes. At the end of the war, the Fairchild C-119 Flying Boxcar that was used in the famous postwar Berlin Airlift took off from Mitchel Field.

Mitchel Field, Mitchel Air Force Command Band. *Courtesy of the Cradle of Aviation Museum of Nassau County Image Collection.*

Secretary of War Stimson and his wife being greeted by officers at Mitchel Field. *Courtesy of the Cradle of Aviation Museum of Nassau County Image Collection.*

This page: An airdrome tractor moving the largest aircraft at Mitchel Field. *Courtesy of the Library of Congress Image Collection.*

Before the formation of the First Air Force Command at Mitchel Field in January 1941, the Sixty-Sixth Fighter Squadron of the Army Air Corps and the Fifty-Seventh Pursuit Group were organized. Organized with the intent of being a defensive force, the squadron was reassigned for overseas combat in the European theater in early 1942. Within three years of being organized, in January 1944, the group became legendary after flying 1,219 missions—totaling 13,476 hours—dropping 2,696,540 pounds of bombs, shooting down 189 enemy aircraft in combat and damaging 84. On April 23, 1944, the Fifty-Seventh Pursuit Group received its biggest citation when it flew a mission between April 1 and 14 over the Florence, Arezzo and Corsica area. The base of the group was the formation of 16 P-47 Thunderbolts, which guided bombers to destroy two tunnels, one railroad bridge, six locomotives, 108 railcars carrying fascist Italian military supplies, 5 motorcade supply vehicles and 40 barrack-like buildings, which crippled the Axis forces in mainland Italy.

While watching planes take off from Mitchel Field and after hearing the heroic stories of the Fifty-Seventh Pursuit Group, locals were inspired by the base's aviation breakthroughs, which were similar to those that had occurred decades prior. This airfield attracted the military's first women pilots and enlistees and some of the legendary Tuskegee Airmen for training. It also transported hundreds of female nurse cadet corps volunteers who left their homes and traditional domestic roles to battlefields, where they earned recognition for their life-saving bravery in caring for Americans who had been injured in combat. Mitchel Field was the first stop for many who braved the elements of the war.

Similar to the media blitz that surrounded the men who signed up for the service, women were encouraged to enlist. The Women Army Axillary Corps (WAAC) was the most aggressive in training and expanding enlistment sites. Adding to its style of recruitment, the WAAC was popularized in the media, which highlighted the sacrifices that women made socially for their country. On May 15, 1942, Franklin Roosevelt signed Public Law 554, creating the WAAC, which was to remain an auxiliary force. In July 1943, America's involvement in the war became more demanding, and the auxiliary forces were moved into fully active status. Once the WAAC obtained active status, *auxiliary* was dropped from its name, and it became known as the WAC (Women's Army Corps). The pay rate for an active member of the WAC was as much as $1.15 per day when average wage was just $0.86 cents a day. The role of an enlisted WAC varied from providing communication support and clerical work to being a part of the air command corps as a test pilot or

Opposite: The controllable pitch housing in the propeller hub at Mitchel Field being adjusted in three of the propellers. *Courtesy of the Library of Congress Image Collection.*

Above: An American pursuit pilot buckles on his parachute just before the takeoff at Mitchel Field. *Courtesy of the Library of Congress Image Collection.*

nurse. The first training center for the WAC was Hunter College grounds in the Bronx. Once the branch was upgraded to fully active status, WACs were trained at Mitchel Field in Garden City and Camp Upton in Yaphank.

The woman responsible for expanding WAC recruitment centers across Nassau County was Lieutenant Frances E. Fallon, one of the first Long Islanders to enlist in the WAC. Lieutenant Fallon also did fifteen-minute segments on the popular radio station WGBB during peak evening hours to highlight the opportunities women could have after enlisting. Following the radio segments, Lieutenant Fallon opened a Rockville Center WAC Center, a Lawrence WAC Center and a Garden City WAC Center. The goal set for the Long Island WACs was fulfill as much of the national enlistment goal of one million women for active service as possible.

Like the male units, the female units were racially segregated. In Hempstead, Bernice Sykes became the first woman to enlist in the colored WAC unit. Becoming the first to sign up, Sykes was put in command of the

Five WACs in matching hats pose together in front of a barrack at Mitchel Field. *Courtesy of the Cradle of Aviation Museum of Nassau County Image Collection.*

Three WACs exiting a gas mask training shack at Mitchel Field. *Courtesy of the Cradle of Aviation Museum of Nassau County Image Collection.*

Colored WAC Hempstead Center. With the public push to fill the national quota of one million women to enlist, local opinion was mixed. In May 1942, *Newsday* posed the question: "Should married women, particularly those with children, enlist in the newly formed WAC?" Out of the five people interviewed, three women and two males, all respondents agreed that no woman with children should sign up for the service. One respondent, Virginia Painter of Old Westbury, stated, "A women's place is in the home, and WAC is especially no place for a mother of a young family."[38] Roger Hussey of Sea Cliff, who was more in support of women in the service, stated, "Husbands leave their wives to go into service, so why shouldn't it be reverse? But women with children should not be allowed to join."[39] This divide in public perception began to shift as more women joined wartime manufacturing. There was a shortage in essential skilled workers, as many male workers had been sent into combat, and the roles of women in the workforce challenged traditional gender roles.

Among the WAC recruits across Long Island, 90 percent volunteered for foreign service, but they were not allowed anywhere near the fighting lines.[40] With the influx of WACs signing up for foreign service, the military expanded women's roles in overseas service with WAVES (Women Accepted for Volunteer Emergency Service or the Women Navel Reserves). The proposal to allow WAVES to go overseas came with a public firestorm in which women's role in war was publicly debated. Congressmen from all over the country voiced their opposition, with representative Jasper Bell stating, "It will be a disgrace to the manhood of this Nation....I do not think that the boys in the armies want young women of our country exposed to fighting."[41]

The congressional pushback affected not only the deployment of female units but also the units' official uniforms. Skirts were required for all women units except for WAFS (Women Auxiliary Ferrying Squadron), which was later known as WASP (Women's Air Service Pilots). Criticism of females' roles in the armed service was not limited to Congress. Many men within the military felt their roles were being challenged and started rumors that enlisted females were lesbians or sexually active with random partners. These rumors were further expanded when tabloids across the New York City area published salacious stories about women becoming pregnant on the front lines, which were all retracted after being proven false. In an effort to combat the negative perceptions of females in the military, Generals Eisenhower and Marshall issued statements of support and strong endorsements of the WAC.[42] Between the media slander and the congressional pushback, the enrollment of women in the armed services was limited to only 150,000, far short of the 1 million women enlistment goal.

The WACs' task at Mitchel Field was to control domestic air traffic above and around Long Island. Trained plane spotters throughout the Nassau and Suffolk Counties would report planes, and WACs would document them and reflect their movements on their maps. This activity was recorded so WACs could look for unusual, unrecognized and unauthorized planes. WACs also served as secretaries and stenographers for all court-martialed proceedings at Mitchel Field. Throughout all the bases where WACs were present, they managed messages from the teletype machine. The teletype was vital because it sent messages from Washington, D.C., to the battlefield and local bases. Operating these machines was done in a centralized communication network that connected moving troops with needed supplies.

At most local aircraft manufacturing companies, WASPs became test pilots. Companies such as Republic had WASPs at the plant conducting daily tests of the Lancer to the Thunder Bolt fighter planes. In total, 1,102 women served as WASPs, and the majority of them were stationed on

Above: Teresa James of the WAFS exiting Republic P-47 cockpit. *Courtesy of the Cradle of Aviation Museum of Nassau County Image Collection.*

Right: Lillian Holmes, an enlisted WAVES, holding a baby. *Courtesy of the Hofstra University Library Special Collection.*

Long Island. To become a WASP, women had to have experience in flying planes or a valid pilot license.

Testing and delivering planes for the service was an essential part of the WASPs' ferry command; their other commands included towing moving air targets for practice. Two of the top starting points for destinations in ferrying planes was Republic Aviation in Farmingdale and Grumman Aviation in Bethpage. The planes were flown by women pilots to air bases as far away as Alberta, Canada. Under the command of Jacqueline Cochran, ten thousand Thunderbolts P-47s were tested and delivered. Cochran, a skilled female pilot who would later be the first female to break the sound barrier, was the most successful WASP when it came to recruitment. One person she recruited was Jean Springer of Babylon. Springer was a trained sea pilot who spent summers flying out from the Babylon Seaplane Base. Springer went on to attend Adelphi University, and during her sophomore year, she signed up for the WASPs. While training, Springer was told to forget anything she previously learned and was trained to fly a Fairchild PT19 and, later, a PT13.[43]

When assigned to the ferrying detail, a WASP's biggest challenge was getting back to home base. Unclear to most military commands was whether WASPs were civilian or military, so many of the pilots were forced take civilian transportation back to their home air bases.

Skilled WASPs were assigned to the most dangerous tasks. Lillian Yonally of Suffolk County, who worked at Grumman, left her job to sign up for the WASP. Yonally's task was to tow target aircraft for antiaircraft practice; these targets were so heavy that, at times, they made the tow plane stall in midair.[44] Even after carrying out these dangerous tasks, women who were killed in action did not receive military burials, honors or benefits. This lack of recognition was due to the WASP being classified as an auxiliary force and not a fully active military service; its main goal was to free up men from domestic air base jobs so they could go to combat. In total, thirty-eight WASPs were killed in action. It was not until 1977 that WASPs received military recognition.

The branch of service with the biggest demand for women was the nurse corps. The United States Nurse Corps during World War II had an estimated 21,000 active female volunteers. The corps struggled to recruit enlistees after the public slander against women in the service. Across Long Island, in Nassau and Suffolk Counties, open-house enrollments for the nurse cadet corps were held in high schools. These open houses were held almost once a month, yielding 868 female senior students for the twenty-three nurse cadet corps training programs across Nassau and Suffolk Counties.[45] To further streamline the nurse cadet program, the director of Adelphi College School of Nursing, Mildred Montag, worked with the high schools in Mepham, Amityville and Farmingdale to incorporate a nursing program for interested seniors. This high school nursing program was then transferable to Adelphi and could be completed in just two semesters. To promote the program, First Lady Eleanor Roosevelt came to Adelphi to dedicate the newly constructed buildings that were to be used for nurse corps training. The total length of the program, from senior year to the two semesters at Adelphi, was eighteen months.

Nurses were needed in domestic military hospitals just as much as they were needed on the front lines. Local media released headlines that stated "Registered Nurses from Nassau and Suffolk Counties Are Needed to Help Meet the Present Nurse Shortage."[46] Another headline in the February 1, 1945 edition of *Newsday* stated, "The Sick Wounded and Helpless Cannot Wait, yet They Must Either Wait or Die, for the Shortage of Nurses Is Becoming Acute, That Drafting of Nurses Has to Be Considered." Nurses were needed in Mason General Hospital in Brentwood and Camp Upton Hospital. To promote the work of these nurses, and in an effort to build a stronger volunteer base, headlines detailed the heroism of the women who braved the face of death to save soldiers.

One nurse, Lieutenant Lucy Wainwright, became known as the "airplane nurse." Wainwright, who was from Oceanside, was the attending nurse on transport flights from the Pacific and European theaters to United States hospitals. Wainwright had a record of serving ninety-seven hours' worth of flights during each year of her service. She was later stationed in Mason General Hospital in Brentwood.[47]

Minneola native Martha Krebs's success in managing the tensions of an overcrowded hospital ward and her hopes of extending her success into combat earned her an army commission. Krebs became known as a Red Cross nurse who managed the New York polio epidemic in Meadowbrook and King County Hospitals; this brought her work to the attention of the military. Once sworn in, she made the rank of second lieutenant and not only was used to manage the military hospitals but also helped in war fund and recruitment drives. Her successful career in managing the polio epidemic and her quick rise through the ranks was used as an example for why quality nurses were needed. In fundraising her most successful war fund drive in Nassau County, between January and March 1945, she set a record for yielding $828,000.

Despite the women who were used as examples of success, women in the service—even as nurses—came with a stigma. To encourage women to join the service and dispel rumors that challenged feminism and females in the service, naval fleet commanders, generals and all military commanders publicly gave statements that said, "Nurse cadet corps does not kill feminine instincts." The Red Cross, understanding the demand for nurses, built a bridge of communication between the enlisted women and their parents. Ruth Holder, the chairperson of the Mineola Recruitment Office, started the Army and Navy Nurses Mothers' Club. The first meeting focused on explaining the role of the cadets and addressing all the negative stereotypes of women who serve. At the first meeting, the members discussed that out of the forty-eight nurses per month, Nassau County only got nineteen new enlistments. The members' other order of business was to petition village courthouses to list the names of women serving in the nurse corps on the honor roll with serving soldiers.[48] Even with all these efforts to enhance enlistment, the nurse cadet corps was unable to fulfill its ambitious quota.

The nurse who became most well known locally was Amityville native Nancy Leftenant. After Nancy graduated from the Lincoln School of Nursing in the Bronx, she was trying to figure out how to serve her country during the war, similar to others in her community. Inspired by her older brother and Tuskegee Airman Samuel Leftenant, Nancy had a desire to serve in the military. But she was concerned about being the only Black nurse to enlist, so she consulted her brother while he was on leave during his airman training. Her brother said, "If you want to go into the military, go. Do not forget what Mom and Dad taught you, and you will not have any trouble."[49] When Nancy enlisted, she became the first Black military nurse in reserve or active duty. Once enlisted, Nancy was sent to train in Camp McCoy in Wisconsin, and then, she was transferred to Fort Huachuca in Arizona. At Fort Huachuca, she cared for Black soldiers and POWs. Following her tour, she served as an air force flight nurse and reached the rank of major before finally retiring in 1965. In her hometown of Amityville, the high school was renamed to honor her service in the military and her pioneering spirit in the civil rights movement.

The army nurse cadets were not exempt from becoming casualties of war. A total of 201 army nurse cadets were killed in action. Florence Evans of Sayville was promoted to the rank of second lieutenant once she was shipped off to the North African campaign. During her deployment, she earned a Bronze Star for bravery and was described as being very gallant in the face of brutal fire fights. During her second deployment into combat,

Evans was killed in Nice, France, in an automobile accident on May 8, 1945. Another decorated nurse who died in combat was Elizabeth Clark of Bay Shore. Clark served as a nurse supervisor in South Side Hospital. She developed a desire to serve following the death of her father, Irwin Clark. Irwin served in the United States Navy and was killed when his aircraft carrier was torpedoed in the Pacific on November 20, 1942. Clark enlisted in the nurse cadet corps and was deployed to the France. She managed nursing operations at the 129th Evacuation Hospital, and while serving in the evacuation hospital, she witnessed the most brutal battles in the European theater. On October 24, 1945, near the end of the war and during occupation operations, Clark was killed in an automobile accident near Frankfurt Germany. Similar to the WASP, it was unclear whether the nurse cadet corps was an extension of the military or civilian service. It wasn't until 2018, when Senator Chris Murphy of Connecticut proposed a bill, that the World War II–era cadet nurses were formally recognized members of the military.

In Long Island and most of New York, racial segregation was enforced either directly or through de facto practices. The rise of the Ku Klux Klan on Long Island further isolated communities of color socially and economically. Building on this isolation was a racial caste system ingrained in stereotypes that Blacks were not equal to Whites. These stereotypes trickled into the armed service. Similar to World War I and wars prior, World War II had racially segregated units. Within these segregated units, many Black soldiers were not trusted by the military command to carry out combat roles. These segregated units persisted until the close of World War II, when President Harry Truman issued Executive Order 9981, integrating every branch of the service. But despite the biases dictated through Jim Crow belief systems, segregated Black units proved themselves on the battlefield. With the rising demand for soldiers, the military had to put some of these biases and racist beliefs aside.

Some of the most distinct Black units that had a strong base on Long Island and New York City were the Tuskegee Airmen and the 92nd and 93rd Infantry Divisions, known as the "Buffalo Divisions." The Tuskegee Airmen unit was started prior to America's involvement in the war, in June 1941. The unit's training took place over a total of eight months, in three ten-week sessions. The total number of Tuskegee Airmen trained was 994. Out of the fewer than 1,000 airmen trained, 450 saw combat; they flew 15,000 missions and received 150 Flying Crosses. These men later became part of the 99th Pursuit Squadron. The first of the squadron to go overseas

Above and opposite: The 332nd Fighter Group Tuskegee Airmen. Collectively, they were awarded 1 Sliver Star, 96 Flying Crosses, 14 Bronze Stars, 744 Air Medals and 8 Purple Hearts. Eight of the airmen were from Long Island. George Arnold Lynch from Valley Stream can be seen standing in the back row in the picture of the men awaiting orders. In the picture of the men working on the plane, Roscoe C. Brown (*right*) had a home in Sag Harbor. *Courtesy of the Library of Congress Photograph Catalog.*

was the 332nd Fighter Group; they flew over in either a Curtis P-40 or Long Island's flagship plane, the Republic P-47 Thunderbolt. Later in the war, the squadron flew the P-51 Mustang. The biggest claim to fame of the Tuskegee Airmen was that they never lost a single bomber to enemy fighters in their two hundred escort missions over Europe.[50] The airmen served on crews for the 477th Bombardment Group that was created in the final year of the war.

Local airman Charles Dryden enlisted on August 19, 1941. Dryden, originally from the Bronx, later graduated from Hofstra University in Hempstead and was stationed at Mitchel Field. He had a strong desire to build a career in aviation. When he was enlisted, Dryden was shipped to Tuskegee Airbase in Alabama for training. While on leave after the completion of his first ten-week training course, Pearl Harbor was attacked. While in his uniform, walking off the train, a person came up to him and said that he should report back to his base because America was under attack. Not understanding what the person was talking about, Dryden headed uptown to see his family in the Bronx. When he reached his family's home, they were crowded around the radio, listening to the news of the Japanese attack on Pearl Harbor. Soon after the attack, Dryden was called back to his base. Originally planned to be used for domestic and a noncombat role, the Tuskegee Airmen were reevaluated following Eleanor Roosevelt's criticism that the army was letting perfectly trained pilots remain on the sidelines because of racial biases. Dryden's training was accelerated, and he was part of the 332nd Fighter Club, the first class to fly into action.

Once deployed, Dryden and the first Tuskegee Airmen were sent to Italy on air-to-ground operations. The first time Dryden encountered a Nazi plane, he was flying in a pack of six Tuskegee Airmen in a P-40 on June 9, 1943. Dryden became excited by the prospect of being the first to shoot down a Nazi plane in his pack. This excitement not only came from the desire for recognition, but it came from a strong desire to show that the Nazi ideology of a supreme Aryan race was false. The best way to prove that was to have a Black person shoot down a Nazi plane. This was

Tuskegee Airman Charles Dyrden, who graduated from Hofstra University and was later stationed at Mitchel Field. *Courtesy of the Hofstra University Library Special Collection.*

not Dryden's last opportunity to shoot down a Nazi, and he was involved in a series of raids against the Italian island of Pantelleria. This series of raids was called the "panty raids" by the airmen. After this series of air-to-ground bombardments, the Nazis surrendered the island. This victory set into motion the airmen's upgrade to the desirable P-47 Thunderbolt for escort missions and the P-51 Mustang for air-to-ground raids.

Despite the bravery of the Tuskegee Airmen in combat, Dryden and the other airmen were not respected by their White counterparts. While on leave, the Tuskegee Airmen were not allowed to attend the same clubs as White soldiers, and White soldiers of lower ranks would not even salute higher-ranked Black soldiers. Glen Cove native William "Joe" Johnson was shocked at the racism he witnessed while training in the South and while deployed among fellow White soldiers. Johnson said, "They talked about racism and whatnot in Germany in Europe, the Nazis. Here, it was bad with lynching, and it was not talked about as a problem among the soldiers."[51] For Dryden, this racism motivated him to take on more dangerous missions,

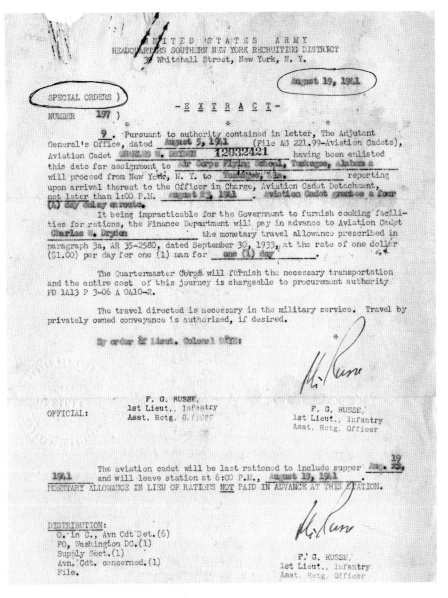

An acceptance letter into the competitive Tuskegee Airmen Training Program dated August 19, 1941. *Courtesy of the Hofstra University Library Special Collection.*

which later earned him the rank of second lieutenant. His determination also earned him a position as a flight instructor at Mitchel Field.

The second deployment of the other Tuskegee Airmen classes included Amityville native Samuel Leftenant, who was stationed on the Ramitelli Air

WAR DEPARTMENT
HEADQUARTERS OF THE ARMY AIR FORCES
WASHINGTON

April 29, 1942

PERSONNEL ORDERS)
NO.   102   )

EXTRACT

14.   Pursuant to authority contained in paragraph 2, Army
Regulations 35-1480, dated November 21, 1932, the following-named
Second Lieutenants, Air Corps Reserve, each of whom holds an aero-
nautical rating, are hereby required to participate in regular and
frequent aerial flights, at such times as they are called to active
duty with the Air Corps, U. S. Army, under the competent authority,
and are authorized to participate in regular and frequent aerial flights,
while on an inactive status, in accordance with the provisions of
paragraph 52, A. R. 95-15, dated April 21, 1930:

            Sidney Paul Brooks
            Charles Walter Dryden
            Clarence Clifford Jamison

    All orders in conflict with this order are revoked.

        By order of Lieutenant General Arnold:

                        J. M. Bevans,
                        Colonel, Air Corps,
                        Director of Personnel.

John H. Wall,
1st Lieut., Air Corps,
Assistant Chief,
Military Personnel Division.

Note: When attached to pay voucher for purpose of collecting flying
        pay this order or true copies thereof, should be in duplicate
        and accompanied by duplicate -
        (a) Copies of order calling the officer to active duty.
        (b) Flight certificate of officer, duly signed by the Commanding
             Officer as called for by existing regulations.

Above: Deployment orders for Charles Dryden to enter active combat duty dated April 29, 1942. *Courtesy of the Hofstra University Library Special Collection.*

Opposite: Dryden's fellow airmen in the 322nd Fighter Group, identified as Byne Sherard, Brown Dart, Leftwich and Laird. *Courtesy of the Hofstra University Library Special Collection.*

Base in Italy. Leftenant was known in his community and at his church, the Bethel AME of Albany Avenue, as a hometown hero. His service inspired others within his community to enlist, including his sister, who signed up for the army nurse cadets. On April 12, 1945, while flying his third mission in his P-51 Mustang over Austria, Leftenant and his flight leader, James Hall, were escorting American bombers that were en route to Germany. Halfway through the mission, Leftenant and Hall's planes collided in midair, and both airmen ejected themselves. Leftenant was never seen again, and the Nazis captured Hall. First, Leftenant was declared MIA (missing in action), but later, in 1946, he was reclassified as KIA (killed in action).

At the close of the war, sixty-six Tuskegee Airmen had been killed in action, and thirty-two had been taken as prisoners of war. The bravery of the Ninety-Ninth Pursuit Squadron became a catalyst for desegregating the branches of the military. Many Tuskegee Airmen carried with them the wounds of the racism, but this motivated them to combat it within their communities. Some Tuskegee Airmen, such as Roscoe Brown of Sag Harbor, went on to become educational activists; Brown even became the president of Bronx Community College. Audley Coulthurst, originally from

Tuskegee Airmen loading bullets into a P-51 Mustang. *Courtesy of the Hofstra University Library Special Collection.*

Jamaica Queens, was part of one of the last classes of Tuskegee Airmen to graduate. Following his service, Coulthurst went on to become a controller for the National Urban League.

The Ninety-Second and Ninety-Third Buffalo Soldier Divisions had their roots in the American frontier, and they had originally been established after the Civil War. The original soldiers from these divisions were former enslaved men who had signed up for opportunities to escape the post–Civil War persecution of Black Americans. Aquebogue native Thomas Watkins, who was the son of a farmworker, suffered discrimination at Riverhead High School. The teachers in Riverhead pushed him away from the idea of going to college and encouraged him to accept a job as groundskeeper. While working as a caddy for the Shinnecock Hills Country Club in South Hampton, Watkins was desperately seeking new opportunities. Similar to the generations of Buffalo Soldiers before him, Watkins signed up for the service to escape the bigotry and racism that limited his opportunities. Following his enlistment, Watkins befriended Huntington native Earl Johnson, who had signed up for the army after the bombing of Pearl Harbor. While they were enlisted, the men did not see combat until the War Department ended its ban on Black soldiers serving in the infantry in active combat.

Watkins and Johnson were the first soldiers of the Buffalo Divisions to see combat. Both men fought in the Arno River in Italy in 1944, which resulted in the legendary actions of John Fox, who saw himself getting overrun by Germans and called an air strike on himself to take out the German troops. This unit sustained heavy casualties, but it played a key role in America defeating the Axis forces in Italy. The actions of this regiment were not officially recognized until 1997, when President Bill Clinton awarded John Fox and six other Black soldiers the Medal of Honor for their bravery in this battle.

At the close of the war, generals who were strongly opposed to Black soldiers fighting in active combat, such as Dwight Eisenhower in the European theater, shifted their views on race. Following the successes of Black fighter squadrons, like the Ninety-Second and Ninety-Third Buffalo Divisions and the Tuskegee Airmen, General Eisenhower became vocal in commending the grit and courage of Black soldiers in combat. In the Pacific theater, General Douglas MacArthur, who had never been opposed the Black fighters, shared the sentiment of Eisenhower that Black soldiers' courage and determination had distinguished them on the battlefield. The brave actions of Black soldiers not only proved racist ideology wrong, but it also disproved the long-held belief that there should be segregated units in the military—in fact, they came to be viewed as liabilities. At the advice of the generals at the close of the war, President Truman issued an executive order to integrate the military. This opened up promotions for many of the Black soldiers who had decided to make the military their career. One man who had a successful military career in the post-integrated service was Tuskegee Airman Charles Dryden. Dryden made the rank of lieutenant colonel, and while stationed at Mitchel Field, he trained a new generation of airmen, White and Black, who fought victoriously in the Korean War.

5

THE WAR OFF THE COAST
OF LONG ISLAND

Making the airspace safe around New York City and Long Island had almost been perfected, but securing the coastline proved to be more of a challenge. Long Island is 118 miles long and 23 miles wide, but it has a coastline that extends 1,600 miles to the north and south. On January 14, 1942, 60 miles off the coast of Montauk Point, Suffolk County, the tanker ship *Norness* was hit by three torpedoes on the starboard side closest to its engine room. The *Norness* was carrying 90,444 gallons of oil that had been chartered by the British Ministry of War Transport. Two sailors drowned while trying to escape to safety. Within a day of the unsuspected attack, 20 miles off the coast of Quogue, Suffolk County, two torpedoes hit a second oil tanker, the *Combria*. The torpedoes punctured the starboard side and hit one of the ship's six main storage tanks, which triggered an explosion. In total, 2 million gallons of oil were lost, and thirty-six crew members were killed.

The devastation of these two tankers had been brought on by Nazi submarine U-123, which was under the command of Reinhardt Hardegen. Hardegen and his crew waged a war along the coast of Long Island, striking fear into all the locals. The sinking of these tankers drew concerns from the navy and coast guard because of how close the U-123 was to the shoreline. The *Combria* sank in thirty-five feet of water, practically hugging the coastline. The *Combria* was so close to the shoreline that Long Beach resident Ruth Fortin recalled, "The water was full of debris and oil slicks from the torpedoed ship—life preservers, broken crates and huge

This page: A Combria oil tanker and bow sinking. It sunk twenty miles off the coast of Quogue, Suffolk County, by Nazi submarine U-123. *Courtesy of the Library of Congress Photograph Catalog.*

pieces of wood littered the beach."[52] Shipping across Long Island came to a temporary standstill, but if this went on for a long stretch of time, it would be devastating to the war effort. New York City and Long Island became the main shipping centers for equipment going to the European theater. U-123 was never caught, and it carried out twelve patrols along the Eastern Seaboard. In total, fifty military ships, merchant ships and commercial oil tankers with 116,000 tons of cargo were either sunk or destroyed by U-123 under the command of Hardegen.

In an attempt to regain control over Atlantic shipping, the United States' warships and planes started patrolling the neutrality zones around New York, which extended six hundred nautical miles around the shoreline.[53] Navy patrols were organized to secure shipping to and from Long Island. Old lifesaving stations that had been vacant for decades became surveillance hubs, and the Montauk and Fire Island Lighthouses had radar stations built in them to detect threats from the ocean and the sky. Along the South Shore towns, locals noticed an influx of Coast Guardsmen. They arrived at all hours of the night and waited by the docks to be transported to Fire Island or to have supplies shipped to the station.

With no time for recreation between shipping goods, the Bay Shore residents met the commander of the Fire Island Coast Guard Station to come up with a resolution. Along the Maple Avenue Docks, community members constructed the United Service Organization Lounge (or USO Lounge). When it was opened in April 1942, the lounge served waiting guardsmen coffee and doughnuts between the hours of 9:00 a.m. and 5:00 p.m. When General Mason Hospital in Brentwood (Edgewood Hospital) got an influx of ferried patients and POWs, the lounge's hours were extended from 9:00 a.m. to 11:00 p.m. During Christmastime, the lounge had presents and held get-togethers for the servicemen. In 1943, as the lounge became a fixture for the enlisted men, the Coast Guard held its 154th anniversary celebration there with a dinner and a dance. The lounge provided leisure activities and little acts of kindness for the servicemen, and the morale of the soldiers was heightened. In addition to the morale boost, the lounge had a section designated for a communication. The radio command section of the building provided a steady network of communication between the Fire Island Station and the mainland for the acquisition of supplies and notification of potential threats.

Western Suffolk was secured by the Fire Island Coast Guard Station, and Eastern Suffolk was secured by the Coast Guard Tiana Station in South Hampton. Military units during World War II were segregated between White and Black soldiers, and a Black unit manned the Tiana Station. An estimated 150 guardsmen were stationed at Tiana, which made it the second-largest guard station to be manned by a Black unit. All of the Black men at the station were from the Manhattan Beach training center and were under the command of chief petty officer Cecil R. Foster. These men ran twenty-four-hour horseback and dog patrols along coastlines and through the brush along the dunes. These patrols were done in an attempt to catch any potential Nazi submarine landings. Unlike the Fire Island Station, the

Bay Shore USO volunteers. *Courtesy of the Bay Shore Historical Society.*

Tiana Station did not have a USO lounge, and the Black soldiers' recreation was confined to baseball teams at the base.

With the growth of these Coast Guard bases along the South Shore, the North Shore of Long Island still had gaps in its security. The overstretched Coast Guard lacked the manpower and boats necessary to provide proper staffing for North Shore stations. In New Suffolk, Southold sheriff Steven Horton was asked to lend his boat for security patrols and the monitoring of U-boat activities. Horton relied on his boat for his livelihood but wanted to contribute to the safety of his community, so he provided a resolution that would be a perfect middle ground. Using his boat and crew, Horton would organize round-the-clock U-boat patrols along the North Shore throughout the duration of the war.

During the peak of the U-boat strikes off the coast of Long Island, Nazi commanders were shifting their methods of attack. On May 26, 1942, U-201 and U-202 set sail from a German base in France en route to America. Both submarines carried eight men who were United States residents but went back to Germany to fight with the Nazis. When they returned to Germany, the men were selected for a secret Nazi mission called Operation Pastorius. The objective of this mission was to sabotage the New York power grid and blow up important bridges, roads and railroad depots. This mission lasted

This page: Tiana Station, seen here in South Hampton, was a segregated unit of the Coast Guard. *Courtesy of the National Archives World War II Collection.*

The Coast Guard used to fly additional patrols between South Hampton and Fire Island, looking for Nazi submarines. *Courtesy of the National Archives World War II Collection.*

for two years and had the goal to create fear domestically in the United States by bringing the war to American soil.

George Dasch, the leader of the eight-man team aboard U-202, had originally resided in New York City and served in the United States Army. Dasch, prior to returning to Germany, took notes on the most important bridges in New York City and the best way to get access to the city's power grid. In the early morning hours of June 13, 1942, U-202 landed off the coast of Amagansett, Suffolk County. George Dasch, Ernst Burger, Richard Quirin and Heinrich Heinck emerged from the vessel and made it to shore with only half of the $175,000 that was provided to them for their terrorist operation. From the fog, Coast Guardsman John Cullen saw the four men coming to the shore during his patrol. Armed with only a flare gun, Cullen called, "Who are you?" One of the men responded, saying they were fisherman who had run aground.[54] Cullen, still visibly unconvinced of the explanation, was startled when Dasch grabbed his arm and shoved a wad of cash into his hand, saying, "Take this, and have a good time. Forget what you've seen here."[55] Cullen then slowly turned around and ran off in the direction of the Coast Guard station.

Within an hour, a full search team descended on the beach and the surrounding area. While the team was searching the shores, the four men hid out in the brush and buried their Nazi uniforms, explosives and other supplies. When daybreak arrived, the men hopped a train from Amagansett Train Station to Penn Station New York City. While the men were on the train, FBI agents stopped it in Freeport and arrested three Norwegian men who they believed were the men who had landed in Amagansett. Following a brief interrogation, the three men were released. While the FBI was distracted, Dasch and his team reached Penn Station, but Dasch, while in transit, reflected on the mission and decided it was impractical.

On June 14, Dasch phoned the FBI and tried to turn himself in. Initially, the FBI believed it was a prank and did not take the call seriously. But the following day, Dasch went into FBI headquarters with documents to confirm his story, which then got the FBI's attention. Ernest Burger, on learning that Dasch was cooperating with the FBI, turned himself in and agreed to cooperate as well. The two other men who had landed with them, Heinck and Quirin, hid out in Astoria at the home of Herman Faje. The two men offered Faje a large sum of the $3,619 they had left over to stay at his home. By June 20, their cover had been blown, and the FBI took them into custody. The four other saboteurs were caught not far from where they landed in Florida on June 20. All of the conspirators were tried and convicted by a military commission. George Dasch and Ernst Burger were spared the death sentence. Dasch was sentenced to thirty years in prison, and Burger was sentenced to life. At the close of the war, President Harry Truman granted a conditional clemency for Burger and Dasch, and they were deported to an American-occupied section of Germany. Herman Faje and his wife, Hildegarde, were indicted and pled guilty in federal court to aiding Nazi spies. In their plea deal, both Herman and his wife were sentenced to five years.

This failed mission was not the last attempt of the Nazi's to organize saboteur missions into America.

As the war progressed, the U-boats' weapons evolved. Missiles that had greater range and could be launched from a submarine out in the ocean were developed. The ranges of the Nazi's V1 and V2 rockets were as far as 250 miles. On January 9, 1945, navy admiral Jonas Ingram estimated that there were three hundred U-boats in the Atlantic and that only six or eight of them were needed to carry out a bombing of New York City from Montauk.[56] With the Nazis desperate for a win following the D-Day invasion of June 6, 1944, an attack or an attempt was expected. Attacks were most likely to occur on a day or night with good weather and clear visibility. After the Nazi landing on eastern Long Island, the army radio corps developed an experimental radio interceptor in Great River, Suffolk County. This radio equipment picked up U-boat messages that gave up their positions; U.S. destroyers and planes then used these messages to locate and destroy the U-boats.[57] The success of the experimental radio equipment led the corps to set up additional equipment along the coastline and at Mitchel Field. Only fifteen seconds of German transmission was needed to pinpoint a U-boat's location.

The radio locating technology experienced its greatest success on January 9, 1944, when Sergeant Theron Jones of Freeport tracked and spotted a German U-boat. His B-25 bomber was loaded with torpedoes and depth charges, and he was ordered to seek and destroy all spotted U-boats. He spotted his target in the Caribbean from five thousand feet and proceeded to destroy the new 750-ton U-boat. With the bombardment of suspected U-boat sites, the vast majority of German submarines retreated from their set patrols along Long Island shores and regrouped for attacks in the mid-Atlantic.

By 1945, U.S. destroyers were equipped with new sonobuoys that had been invented the year prior. Developed as a shared wartime technology for the Royal and American Navies, the sonobuoys became game changers for tracking U-boats. On April 5, 1945, a navy destroyer, USS *Otter*, successfully tracked a German submarine along the Atlantic Coast and into the mid-Atlantic, where it blew it up. The third and final U-boat sunk two months after being identified while sending a weather transmission on May 6, 1944. The USS *Croatan* tracked U-853 up the coast of Massachusetts, but then, it disappeared. The crew of the *Croatan*, disturbed by how close U-853 was to the shore, formed an obsession with destroying it. On June 17, 1944, the boat was spotted surfacing by a fighter plane. The *Croatan* sailed over to the location, only to find that the boat had disappeared again. The crew nicknamed the U-boat "Moby Dick" and the determined U.S. Navy captain John Vest captain "Ahab."[58] On May 6, 1945, just ten miles south form Block Island, U-853 met its demise. This was the closest a German submarine was sunk to the Long Island shore during World War II. Following the sinking of the submarine, local papers described the location of its sinking as ironic, due to its proximity to Nantucket Port,

World War II B-25 aircraft being loaded with bombs at Mitchel Field for an antisubmarine mission. *Courtesy of the Cradle of Aviation Museum of Nassau County Image Collection.*

which was the home port of the fictional Captain Ahab. Today, U-853 still sits under 130 feet of water with all fifty-five of its crew members at their battle stations. Due to its popularity among treasure hunters and to preserve the site as a wartime grave site, navy divers welded the holes that caused the U-boat to sink in an effort to keep hobby divers out.

The destruction of these submarines showed the Germans that their once-stealthy attacks were things of the past. Fortunately, the threats and dire warnings caused by an enemy that lurked hundreds of feet in the water did not result in any faltering of Long Island's support or mobilization for the war. Nazi resources were stretched too thin for any organized attacks close to American shores, but random acts of terrorism were affordable. Smaller-scale operations were encouraged and funded by Nazi agents. The famous troop carrier *Normandie* (a former luxury liner that had a transfer of ownership to the U.S. Navy, which renamed it *Lafayette*) caught fire in the New York City Harbor. Due to the anxiety of the U-boat attacks and the symbolism of the historic ship, many believed it was sabotage. Following an investigation, it was concluded that the ship caught fire on accident during routine maintenance. But a one-time German resident of Long Island, Fritz Scheffer, claimed he supervised the workers who started the

African American seamen delivering shells and loading the antiaircraft gun aboard a vessel on the Atlantic patrol that was looking for the last of the four Atlantic Nazi submarines. *Courtesy of the New York Public Library.*

fire that destroyed the ship.[59] Scheffer claimed he was part of a greater sabotage ring. On further investigation, it was found that Scheffer was an active member of the German Bund, which had connections to Nazi spy rings. His confessions and account of the fire were not investigated further, but many believe he was telling the truth.

6.

ARSENAL FOR DEMOCRACY

Wartime Manufacturing

With the rise of Hitler and antisemitism, Albert Einstein fled Germany and settled in New Jersey after taking a position at Princeton University. While in New Jersey, Einstein established a second home in Southold, Suffolk County, on Old Grove Road. This second home gave him time to reflect and correspond with other scientists who were still in Germany. After receiving updates from his fellow scientists, Einstein found out that Nazi Germany was seeking the ability to create a uranium-based bomb. Following late-night conversations with quantum physicists Leo Szilard and Eugene Wigner in which the men discussed Germany's ability to develop such a bomb, Einstein and his fellow scientists developed a shared fear. With the scientists and resources Germany had accumulated during its recent invasions, it became Einstein's top priority to bring awareness of this mega bomb threat to the highest levels of American government.

On August 2, 1939, from his Southold home, Einstein wrote a letter to President Roosevelt, stating that Germany could use "large quantities of new radium-like elements that would generate a nuclear chain reaction which could be constructed into a bomb, carried in a boat that can explode not just a port but an entire surrounding territory." Einstein went on to further explain that Hitler's invasion of Czechoslovakia was a dire warning, as the country possessed uranium ore that could be mined, but he said the "Belgian Congo would have the larger source to make such a bomb." The letter was a wake-up call for America to start militarizing as fast and aggressively as possible. Federal grants for defense contracting, the rationing

HEMPSTEAD
WAR BOOK

Hempstead War Book cover. This book was given out to village residents to promote war bond purchases. *Courtesy of the Hofstra University Library Special Collection.*

of products that could make weapons, fundraising for an arsenal of democracy, freeing up potential manufacturing line workers and, most important of all, building on innovative ideas for new weapons to neutralize such threats were priorities. All of these inspired vehicles of militarization were in the shadow of Roosevelt's ultimate decision that changed the course of human history: to develop the Manhattan Project, which paved the way for a functioning nuclear bomb.

Civilian defense efforts were not limited to vigilance and preparation for attacks. New York State governor Herbert Lehman, understanding the severity of the war, passed the War Emergency Act, which provided state resources to form local, community-based war councils within the state. The community councils reported to a state field representative to make sure their goals and visions were aligned with the needs of the war effort. Rallying the communities behind the war effort by encouraging them to buy war bonds and conserve and participate in metal drives was essential to wartime production.

The Hempstead War Council generated awareness around the importance of buying war bonds. The council posted government-provided war bond posters all over the village and gathered business sponsors to not only help advertise the bonds but to be vendors for them. Franklin Square National Bank, the People's National Bank and Trust of Lynbrook, the First National Bank and Trust of Freeport and the First National Bank of Merrick grossed some of the highest sales of war bonds in Long Island. The banks and the Hempstead War Council advertised the bonds as "the best and safest investment in the world, with a return of $4 for every $3 at maturity."[60] In the first year of the war, 1942, war bond sales for Nassau County netted $19,000,000; the following year, they netted $23,000,000; and in the third year, they shattered all goals and generated $29,998,500.[61] More creative methods to raise money for the war effort included the Hempstead War Council's shows at the Rivoli Theatre in downtown Hempstead. The money raised at the shows was sent to an emergency relief account.

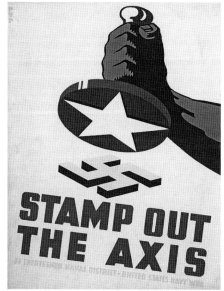

Throughout all of Long Island's downtown banks, townhalls and other businesses, posters were hung to promote civilian war efforts. *Courtesy of the Library of Congress Photograph Catalog.*

With the progression of the war, raw materials were in higher demand. The standard economic principals of supply and demand increased the prices of everyday and essential goods. To prevent inflation and balance supply with demand, President Franklin Roosevelt issued Executive Order 8734, which created the Office of Price Administration and Civilian Supply. Prices were frozen for just under 90 percent of all household goods, but it also implemented a rationing of most consumer products throughout the war. One of the most important materials to ration was oil and gasoline. As oil was vital for transportation on the warfront, keeping factories online for twelve to eighteen hours a day was a challenge for Long Island.

Long Island winters, similar to most in the Northeast, can be brutal, and they raised the home heating oil demand. Ration limits for residential units were based on the number occupants and square footage of the house, but babies and illnesses among occupants were considered when creating the supply quota. Across Long Island, heads of households inflated their household size and lied about special requirements of illnesses. This created a rule that all illness exemptions must be accompanied by a certification from a doctor as to the temperature required for proper care of any sick person in the household.[62]

A Grumman Wildcat airplane was exhibited at Columbus Circle for bond selling purposes. *Courtesy of the Library of Congress Photograph Catalog.*

Following the heating oil reform, newly appointed Nassau County rationing administrator Augustus. B. Weller put a county ban on pleasure driving to set county limits on gas usage. Driving was only unconditional when done for business, shopping and traveling between old and new residences.[63] Similar to the community pushback on fuel oil rationing, Nassau County residents petitioned elected officials that the rationing of gas was unfair, as no driving limits had been set in New York City, and the county had been developed around the car. Seeking an opportunity, illegal gas stamp rings were formed. John Skillen, Edward Morris and Ted Cotler of Long Beach bought stamps from inactive cab drivers and sold the rations for a dollar a stamp.[64] The trio's stamp ring was the largest in the county, and a total of ten thousand gallons' worth of rationed gas stamps were seized at the time of their arrest. Despite the outcries and illegal black markets for gas stamps, the county's residents begrudgingly complied with the limits set on car usage.

By 1943, the federal government had put a quota on local villages to raise scrap metal. Rockville Center had a quota to collect 700,000 pounds of scrap metal per year. The established quota came with the appointment of George Serenbetz to the newly formed Nassau Salvage Committee. A goal of 125 pounds of metal for all five thousand homes across the village of Rockville Center was proposed. This goal was advertised as enough metal to build thirty-five tanks.[65] Prior to this quota, Rockville Center was collecting 80,000 pounds of metal during its spring salvage and scrap metal drive. To obtain the new quota, historic ornamental cannons that been decommissioned following the Spanish-American War and placed in front of American Legion Halls, parks and village greens were turned over to be melted down and made into new weapons.

Prices were frozen on 90 percent of all household goods, which implemented rationing on most consumer products throughout the war. One of the most important materials to ration was oil and gasoline. The ration books kept track of the daily limits on these essential goods. *Courtesy of the Library of Congress Photograph Catalog.*

Overall, a majority of Long Island's residents supported the scrapping efforts and embraced the quotas within their households, but some small businesses were in strong opposition. In 1942, Harry Gudkin, the owner of an automobile junkyard in East Islip (across from modern-day Friendly's Ice Cream on Main Street), refused to turn over any of his metal for the Bay Shore scrap metal salvage drive. Gudkin, for months, was publicly shamed by his peers and harassed daily by local rationing administrators, but he continued his refusal to participate. Gudkin's opposition was further investigated by the Farm Security Administration, but by the time violations were drawn up, the wartime scrap and rationing drives were over. Unlike Gudkin, the majority of Long Islanders embraced this sense of civic duty and set records that surpassed scrap metal goals in the other surrounding metro areas of New York City.

The success of the scrap metal drives inspired oil and fat salvage drives. Residents across Nassau and Suffolk Counties and the five boroughs of New York City were encouraged to save all cooking oil, grease and fats. The government had an overall goal of raising 200 million tons of fats. In 1942, a short-term national goal of 15,050,000 pounds of fats, grease and cooking oils was established. These numbers were modest when compared to a government study that concluded Americans used and disposed of 2 billion pounds of fats, oils and grease a year. The kitchen waste was used to produce glycerin, a fat-based byproduct that makes explosives such as nitroglycerin, during the war. One pound of this fat made one pound of explosives. Edward McDonough was appointed to head the fat salvage drives in Nassau County, Long Island, and in his first year, he had 50 percent of all households participating.

On August 18, 1943, McDonough gave a detailed interview to *Newsday*, stating, "Fats and oils are important to not only building explosives but in medicine. Sulfa-based drugs have been widely publicized as life savers, but few people realize that cooking grease can be used to make surgical dressings."[66] A supply of fats could also be utilized to process plasma for blood transfusions; a single pound of fat could process 260 quarts of blood.[67] Fats from one hundred thousand households in Nassau County could provide plasma transfusions for one day's worth of patients in the European theater. This interview created the sense of urgency that was needed to grow the program. The second year of the fats drive in Nassau County only yielded 87,165 pounds, but by the third year, the collection had increased to 97,077 pounds. An estimated 70 percent of the Nassau County's population participated in saving fats for the war effort.[68] The

Bay Shore scrap metal drive. *Courtesy of the Bay Shore Historical Society.*

wartime demands for fats extended not only into preserving used fats but also in using substitutes in cooking recipes. To conserve store-bought shortening, which was rare due to rationing, homemakers were encouraged to make their own shortening with pig fat.[69] Unlike other salvage programs in different regions throughout the country, Nassau and Suffolk Counties had some of the highest participation rates.

Though raw materials and money were put in place by local civilian defense organizations, they were only part of the solution for the war effort. Unlike the decade prior, Long Island had a strong demand for manufacturing jobs. Nationwide, 16 million people were serving in the armed services. In New York State, the total population was 13.4 million, with an estimated 1 million peak-working-age residents serving in the armed forces. Prior to America entering World War II, President Roosevelt amended the Neutrality Acts of 1937, which prohibited America from intervening with the sales of any supplies to nations in conflict, with a "cash and carry" policy. Cash and carry allowed the sales of supplies for civilian use, but the country buying the goods had to pay cash and pick it up itself. *Civilian supplies* were vaguely defined.

Grumman of Bethpage, utilizing the vague definition, placed bids to fill English warplanes with mounts for—potentially—six machine guns. The best feature of these planes was the new Wright Cyclone motor. The Wright Cyclone stood out from all other motors because of its ability to fly at the top speed of 330 miles per hour for a distance of 1,000 miles. Fairchild

Aircraft of Farmingdale won bids for planes and other equipment that did not include guns and soon expanded production hours. For Grumman and Fairchild, sales went from $3,977,000 in 1938 to $4,400,000 in 1940, but they had additional $6,000,000 in back-logged sales.[70]

With the expanding industry and a growing economy and Axis threat, Roosevelt signed into law House Bill 1776, or the Lend-Lease Program. This law openly permitted the sales of military equipment to Allied countries. With many of the military contracts in place, the Long Island aircraft industry started setting sales and profit records. By 1941, nationwide exports to England had increased from $504,000,00 to $991,000,000. Asian countries matched this demand, with China as America's biggest customer, purchasing $77,000,000 in exports. By 1941, all plane manufacturers were employing three times as many people per week as they had the previous year, according to the Aeronautical Chamber of Commerce.[71]

Predicting an even larger aircraft manufacturing boom, Grumman, Liberty and Republic started expanding and building new facilities. Grumman, located in Bethpage, built an additional plant that needed 16,000 workers, 8,000 of them mechanics. This new 1,200,000-square-foot facility was a $2 million investment for Grumman, but this plant was dwarfed by Liberty's and Republic's facility expansions in Farmingdale. By 1945, Long Island had 100,000 aircraft manufacturing jobs, with Republic Aviation and Grumman employing the majority of the 100,000 positions. Geographically, Long Island had a new innovative highway system built close to the established railroad lines; Long Island was also surrounding by ocean, which gave it an advantage in maritime shipping. But the largest challenge to mass production in Long Island was its working-age population, which numbered only 250,000 in both Nassau and Suffolk Counties. In an attempt to get workers from Queens and Brooklyn, which had much larger populations, became a challenge, as hundreds of thousands of wartime manufacturing jobs were already located in the city. One large wartime employer in the city was the Brooklyn Navy Yard, which employed 71,000 people throughout the war.

Across Long Island, there were thousands of sixteen- to seventeen-year-old high school kids who were capable of meeting the physical demands of working in a defense plant, but they were enrolled in high school. This untapped potential made high schools go through an almost full reprograming of their basic curriculum in most subjects to fit in manufacturing plants' hours of operation. To attract this group to defense plant jobs, New York State formed the youth service councils throughout Long Island high schools.

The two main goals of this group were to promote war activities of youth and motivate youth to set career goals around vocational jobs in defense plants.[72] Encouraging interest in defense manufacturing among adolescents came with a drastic change in secondary education through the elective courses the schools offered. New York State wanted students to have a basic knowledge of the machinery utilized in manufacturing plants so that they could become active in the war effort.

The mass mobilization of the navy came with challenges in training to identify the differences between a hostile plane and a friendly plane. Similar to other problems, finding solutions came in secondary school programing and the mobilization of adolescents. The use of spotter models (a small-scale model of planes) in training to identify the different aircrafts were direly needed. Each spotter model was a replica of what the plane would look like, but the problem was that the Defense Department needed 500,000 of these models to reflect the different kinds of aircraft around the world. The federal government picked thousands of school districts across the country—and most of the districts in Nassau and Suffolk Counties and all of the city's five boroughs—to add model plane making in the curriculum. The navy set a 60,000-plane quota for selected schools, which included specifications to the planes that needed to be completed in the first year.[73] In March 1943, New York State published a booklet that identified the planes the students would make and how the program would be rolled out in mandatory high school shop classes.

Within the model plane–building mandate rollout in high school programing innovation was fostered through imagination and led to new inventions in aviation. During a model plane–building competition, Charles Daly of Garden City took first prize with his detailed model of Grumman's Gulf Hawk, which took an estimated two years to make. Liberty Aircraft was so impressed that they took notice, and to their surprise, he invented a new divider for manufacturing. Daly was quickly assigned a patent lawyer and offered an engineering job at Liberty Aircraft.

To further free up the potential in youth labor, New York State had high school programing change to accommodate working students. New York high schools adopted classes that were taught after work hours, and depending on their job, students could receive class credit for the work they did in the defense plant.[74] This programing and part-time job internships provided guaranteed full-time jobs once students left high school.

In an attempt to further extend the full labor potential of the state, Governor Lehman created the Discrimination in Employment Committee in early 1941. Despite the efforts of locals, the labor pool was not matching the demand in defense jobs. Wartime manufacturing could not afford to discriminate. On June 25, 1941, President Roosevelt issued Executive Order 8802, which prohibited racial discrimination in all defense industries and all private companies under government contract. This executive order freed up resources for New York to make the state discrimination committee and form a compliance board to replace the inquiry committee that was in place prior to the order. Aligned with the federal order, the committee only focused on defense plant jobs, defense manufacturing based unions and defense training schools. The committee's appointed chairpersons were Frieda Miller and, later, Alvin Johnson, who organized investigations in hiring practices that prevented people from getting hired based on race, color, national origin and ancestry. The federal mandate and committees, such as New York State's Discrimination Committee, created the largest employment gains for Black women in industrial occupations, which reflected a rise from 6.5 percent to 18.0 percent employment, and an overall 40.0 percent wage increase for all labor demographics across defense industry positions.[75]

On April 8, 1943, the state discrimination board faced one of its many tests in Nassau County. Black men and women were completing aviation programs and were not getting hired. One defense plant (not named) had 533 employees but employed only 8 Black people. Several people filed a discrimination complaint, stating that "after they completed courses in defense schools, they had been given a runaround by war plants, or refused to hire them without explanation."[76] A series of these complaints put most of the Long Island defense plants under routine monitoring for their hiring practices. The efforts of the state monitoring and legislation paved the way for Grumman to hire over 800 Black men and women, which made up 3.3 percent of the Grumman Bethpage workforce. This number was a milestone for the committee because it reflected the demographic of Nassau County, whose citizens of color made up 3.0 percent of the population. While monitoring local plants, regulators received complaints of Jewish people being dismissed on grounds of security concerns. The state took notice and extended the discrimination regulations to include religious groups. The council's work was able to free up some of the labor pool that was needed, but there was still a demand that exceeded the number of available workers.

Demand for workers put women front and center when filling aircraft manufacturing jobs. Headlines in local papers read, "If Enough Fighters and Torpedo Bombers Are to Reach Our Boys in the Pacific and European Fronts, the Wives, Mothers, Sisters and Sweethearts Are Going to Have to

Help Build Them."[77] Traditionally, women did not work in aircraft and ammunition manufacturing plants, but similar to World War I, during World War II, women became an essential labor pool. Throughout the war, women held 25 percent of all aircraft and defense manufacturing positions. This number reflected only a 10 to 15 percent increase of women in wartime manufacturing positions by the end of the war.

An overwhelming majority of women workers who did fill the wartime manufacturing positions were women who had previously been in the labor force, but cutbacks during the Great Depression had forced them to drop out. Dropping out of the workforce led these women to get back into domestic work or settle into full-time motherhood. During World War II, employers, unlike what they had done during World War I, attempted to attract women to war jobs by focusing on what kept women out of the labor force. The biggest challenge that kept young working-age women out of the labor force was childcare.

The New York State War Council estimated the state would need 250,000 women to fill its various wartime manufacturing positions. The state, in 1942, formed the Committee on Childcare Development and Protection, which had the goal of forming a preschool as a means of childcare to free women up for work.[78] The passage of the federal Lanham Act provided the state with $3 million in yearly federal grants to fund childcare. Community war councils were assigned to train as many preschool teachers and childcare providers as possible in a short amount of time. In Hempstead, the local war council and Work Progress Administration supervisor for education, Jane Oakes, set up a ten-week course to train childcare providers; these courses were held in the Red Cross Office located at 111 Front Street in Hempstead. The course's content included better ways to cope with the effects of the strains and stresses of the war on adults and children.[79] In addition to providing social and emotional learning for children, these early childcare programs, which were sponsored by the state grants, had the goal of providing light early academic foundations for children to help them transition to elementary-level education.

To help fill its demand for workers, Grumman Aircraft Manufacturing opened its own childcare center for its female employees in Freeport. This company's daycare site provided childcare for children between the ages of six and fourteen. Children who were under the age of six were sent to temporary home cares at private residences that were paid for by Grumman.[80] The demand for employees and daycare forced Grumman to open up a second childcare program in Suffolk County with split day and night sessions. This program allowed not only women who worked during the day but also those who went to night school training for jobs that included riveting, welding and sheet metal work to enroll their kids.[81] Unlike the war council's childcare program's original centralized goal of social and emotional learning, Grumman's childcare program only expanded its curriculum to include academics and community-based field trips.

With workplace daycares put in place, air defense companies established annual family days. This day became an event that allowed women workers to take their children to work and show them what they built. Republic Aviation in Farmingdale had the largest family days, which attracted fifty-seven thousand people at their peak in 1943. Invited to Republic's family day were the children and family members of its workers. During these events, Republic attempted to lure its workers' other working-age family members to apply for jobs. With all the childcare programs and efforts to encourage women to apply for defense jobs, a total of twenty thousand women across Long Island filled these positions.

Harnessing a traditionally untapped labor pool came with a demand for training. The defense plants were in need of a highly skilled labor

A poster promoting women getting jobs in defense plants and other essential wartime jobs. *Courtesy of the Library of Congress Photograph Catalog.*

The Republic Aviation Corporation ID badge of Josephine Rachiele. Josephine took a training course and got a job with Republic Aviation. *Courtesy of the Cradle of Aviation Museum of Nassau County Image Collection.*

force. If workers were not properly trained, the production line could be dangerous, and it could prove fatal for the people who were operating the planes and weapons on the battlefield. Prior to the war, the state education department predicted an increased demand in aircraft manufacturing and defense contracting. By 1941, England was ordering aircrafts and electronic aircraft parts from Bethpage Grumman. Filling these orders required skilled labor, but there were limited training facilities. Federal funds from the National Youth Administration geared the training programs for young men and women between the ages of seventeen and twenty-five. One of the few training schools in the state was the Roosevelt

Aviation School at Roosevelt Field. The school was effective but took two years to complete. A successful training program had to be streamlined with an accelerated curriculum. The New York State Department of Education, understanding the potential boom in aviation schools, set up a standard for admittance into these new programs. The new standards included being a grammar school graduate, being over the age of eighteen years and passing a written aptitude test from the state.[82] Streamlining these requirements would not only increase admission but also provide a baseline to create a unified curriculum.

Grants from the federal and state governments were too time consuming, and many aviation companies, like Ranger, Republic, Columbia and Grumman, opened their own various training schools. Columbia paid trainees to attend its school on a split schedule. The training campus, located 190 Earle Ave Lynbrook, offered class sessions from 8:00 a.m. to 4:30 p.m. and part-time sessions from 7:00 p.m. to 9:00 p.m., with an optional extension to midnight. This training covered the basics in aircraft manufacturing and factory safety. For more highly skilled engineering jobs, Adelphi created an engineering, science and management program. This program, unlike similar degree programs that lasted two to four years, was consolidated into just eight weeks.

To further streamline the training programs, factories funded schools that focused on specific trades that were needed on assembly lines instead of providing a complete overview of defense manufacturing. The Faust Aircraft Sheet Metal Training School advertised a trade program that was designed for sheet metal assembly line workers, which had Republic fund as much as $250,000 to extend the program with the promise to deliver five thousand graduates by the end of 1941.[83] In adopting the trade-based model, Ranger Aircraft teamed up with Fairchild to create a two-week program. This school recruited high school students, disabled people and women, as well as late-working-age men. Grumman, almost in competition for skilled workers, created a three-hundred-hour training course for neighborhood schools. Sewanhaka was home to the first Grumman sheet metal and glider construction program.

To advertise the skills that were acquired from the various training schools, defense manufacturing expos were organized. Adelphi University held the largest of these expos; there, companies showed off defense industry technology and provided open houses for job applicants. During the expo, competitions were held to show off workers' skills, including one to show how many rivets could be put into sheet metal within five minutes. The booths

Bay Shore Aviation School. This trade school was funded by Grumman and Republic in an effort to get skilled workers in the aircraft factories. *Courtesy of the Bay Shore Historical Society.*

in these expos became bragging opportunities for companies; in them, they showed off what they were doing for the war effort and advertised their civilian-use products.

The cultural shift in skilled programs and the returning students, who were, in many cases, housewives, shifted local commerce. Local supermarkets stayed open later to accommodate working women. Newspapers and magazines, which once had advertising targeted toward men, shifted to have products and services advertised toward women. Mortgage lenders, for the first time, targeted women and had them portrayed in advertising as heads of households.

Money, resources and a growing labor pool left only innovation as a key component in competing defense contracts. Grumman, Republic and Seversky, Liberty, Ranger, Brewster, Columbia and Sperry witnessed growth that outpaced production. Company headquarters that were once surrounded by countryside or large sections of the Hempstead Plains transformed into bustling towns to accommodate the economic growth of the manufacturing plants. The landscape of Long Island was changing drastically. Farmland was developed and transformed into airfield landing strips. Once-vacant marshland in eastern Queens was drained to accommodate a 1,000-acre airport (which later became JFK International Airport). Western Suffolk County Civil Aeronautics purchased 850 acres in the town of Islip in 1942. The following, year 200 more acres were purchased to extend the airport along Lincoln Avenue in Ronkonkoma. The combined 1,050 acres was leased out in 1944 to Sperry Gyroscope Company in an effort to have the company use the runways to test their new innovations for American combat aircraft. After the war, this airport was renamed MacArthur Airport or, as locals refer to it, Islip Airport.

Established construction and manufacturing companies switched over to wartime production to take advantage of the lucrative contracts that were provided to them. In an effort to cash in on the new wartime production, startups rose up from the potato farms of Nassau and Suffolk Counties. One example of these wartime startups was the Long Island Motor Works of Sayville. This company was a subcontractor of Republic and Grumman Aviation. Motor Works exclusively produced landing gears that were later assembled in Grumman Wildcats, Hellcats, Avengers and Republic P-47 Thunderbolts.

Some companies, such as Dzus Fastener Company, reinvented their peacetime products for the wartime production. Dzus constructed fasteners for tractors and other pieces of agricultural equipment, but with the increased demand for aircraft, the company remarketed its fasteners for the fighter planes constructed by Grumman and Republic. Dzuz became so busy in backorders that they ran the factory for eighteen hours a day and ballooned to five hundred employees. Smith Marine Service of Islip switched over from boat repair to the mass production of tools and the rubber bushings that were installed in all bombers for Republic Aviation.

Brewster's Shipyard of Bay Shore operated for over one hundred years while providing the same service, but all of its traditional clients' needs were put on hold during the war. Brewster's built forty-six army tugboats and ten 110-foot barges that were designed to ship cargo and weapons. Becoming the biggest shipyard in Long Island, Brewster expanded its machine shops to service Grumman aircraft parts. Later, it became the exclusive contractor for all repairs of the military boats that were utilized in the New York area.

Similar to Brewster, maritime manufacturer Sculler Safety Manufacturing Corporation of Lindenhurst made rafts for pleasure boats but switched over exclusively to defense manufacturing during the war. Sculler Corp. modified its previous products of emergency rafts to amphibious planes for the navy fleet. The navy and air corps contracts were so large that a production facility had to be expanded into the old West Babylon School, which had been abandoned years prior.

Dade Brothers Factory Interior, located by Roosevelt Field, received one of the largest contracts for a small, independent Long Island company. The contract was to construct the CG-4 troop glider. Dade Brothers', prior to the war, was a homebuilding company, and it was not the top choice for the government contract. Steinway and Sons Piano Company had the contract but could not fill the order, which was then handed over to Dade Brothers.[84] This wood-based glider was designed to carry a dozen of troops and up to 7,500 pounds of cargo while being towed and released behind enemy lines. Its top speed while towing was 150 miles per hour, and once it was cut, it was made to cruise at 70 miles per hour. The drawback of the glider was that it had to be towed at night in order to be stealthy. When released behind enemy lines, the Germans would put black-painted telephone poles up in an attempt to get the gliders to crash into them while landing.

The smaller-scale production of parts was done by companies such as Columbia Aircraft. Founded by aviator Charles Levine and aircraft designer Giuseppe Mario Bellanca, Columbia established its manufacturing plant in Mineola. Charles Levine's creditability in aviation was based on him being the first Jewish American pilot. Their work was centered on amphibian planes. The company's most well-known plane was the J2F-6 Duck, and a total of 584 were built. The top speed of the J2F-6 was 190 miles per hour for a range of 790 miles. The biggest selling point of the J2F-6 was its ability to land and take off on a body of water. The company's next model was XJL-1, but only three were produced. This plane was the first single-winged amphibian plane. The low production number was due to the plane being manufactured in mid-1945. When the third plane was rolled out from the production line, the war was over—along with the demand for this plane.

The top-level management of Columbia Aircraft was devastated after the arrest of cofounder Charles Levine. In early 1942, Levine was arrested for smuggling a Jewish refugee named Edward Schinek, who escaped a

The Dade Brothers production of CG four Gliders. In this image, six women can be seen working on partially constructed aircraft. *Courtesy of the Cradle of Aviation Museum of Nassau County Image Collection.*

concentration camp, into America across the Mexican border. Grumman later took over the production line under the management of John Kenny. Expanding the company's production required more land for testing the planes. In the summer of 1942, Columbia Aircraft took over the old defunct Curtiss Airfield in Valley Stream. The economic boom that occurred after Grumman took over production was only temporary. The close of the war marked the end of Columbia Aircraft.

The tightest competitors with the greatest impact on Long Island culture was Grumman and Republic Aviation. The strength of both companies was in their innovative engineers and managers, which included Jake Swirbul and Alexander Kartveli. Jake Swirbul, a native to Sag Harbor Long Island, was introduced to Leon Grumman in the early 1920s at an airshow. Both were Long Island natives and passionate about the future in aviation. They became the main drivers in creating Grumman Aircraft Corporation. During the war, Swirbul's management style created effective employee loyalty and productivity. Swirbul's goals were not centered on having his employees

Liberty Aircraft Corporation in Farmingdale, a smaller defense plant competitor to Republic and Grumman. *Courtesy of the Library of Congress Photograph Catalog.*

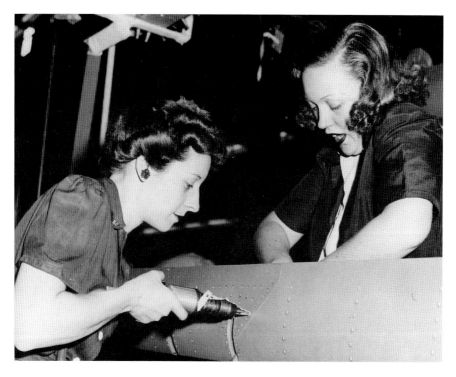

Two women riveting at Liberty Aircraft. *Courtesy of the Cradle of Aviation Museum of Nassau County Image Collection.*

A Columbia Aircraft XJL-1; only three were produced. The war ended before full-scale production. *Courtesy of the Cradle of Aviation Museum of Nassau County Image Collection.*

focused on the short-term goals of production; instead, he wanted them focused on the guiding idea that America needed them in the war. The ten-hour workdays of these workers could be vexing, but the managers under Swirbul created baseball teams that competed with other manufacturers, building company loyalty and fun competition among rival companies. Additionally, managers would remind employees of the company's guiding ideas and the effectiveness of carrying them out by keeping track of how many enemy planes their planes were shooting down each week. All these elements created the environment needed to set records in the production of aircraft and to keep innovative ideas flowing.

The most well-known planes that Grummans produced were the Wildcat, the Hellcat and the Avenger. Wildcat F4F was Grumman first mass-produced monoplane. Originally produced before the war for the American and Royal Navies, the plane was innovative for its time. The Wildcat's top speed was 331 miles per hour with a range of 830 miles. In total, 7,885 Wildcats were produced, but a majority of the American fleet of Wildcats were grounded following the attack on Pearl Harbor on December 7, 1941. The handful that were operational were the first to defend America against Japan in the

Executive Leroy Grumman (*right*) poses with Jake Swirbul (*left*) and actor Robert Taylor as he holds a model of a Grumman plane. *Courtesy of the Cradle of Aviation Museum of Nassau County Image Collection.*

Pacific. Holding the line against the Japanese AM6M Zero fighter planes, the Wildcat was almost evenly matched on performance. But following the attack on Pearl Harbor, America had to show Japan that it could rise up from the ashes of the Pearl Harbor attack bigger and stronger.

In an attempt to make a plane that could outperform the Japanese Zero, Queens-based Brewster aviation developed the F2A Buffalo. The top speed of the Brewster F2A Buffalo was 321 miles per hour, but it had a sluggish pick up. Flyers complained, "The Japanese Zero fighter can run circles around the Brewster Buffalo that had been a hand down, with wheel struts which broke during hard landings."[85] Following the embarrassment of the F2A, the Pacific fighter planes needed improved performance, durability and fast production.

The Hellcat F6F became the answer and the flagship plane for Grumman. The birthplace of the Hellcat was Bethpage, Long Island, and it rose through the ranks to become a hometown hero. This plane wove itself into a symbol of Long Island pride. The Hellcat was brought into production in early 1943. Its top speed was 380 miles per hour with a range of 944 miles. The plane stood out due to its large wingspan of forty-three feet, which folded for storage on aircraft carriers. Its weapons included six Browning machine guns, which could hold four hundred rounds of ammunition, and it had the ability to carry a two-thousand-pound bomb. The plane's best feature was its cost. The Grumman Hellcat cost was $35,000, as compared to the similar Vought Corsair navy fighter, which cost between $57,000 to $72,000 per plane.[86]

The price and performance of the Hellcat F6F had a demand that matched its production. Bethpage Grumman produced an average of 450 of the Hellcats a month, producing a total of 12,275 by the end of the war. In 1944, the groundbreaking invention of the Al-Fin process was applied to later Hellcat models. The Fairchild Airplane Corporation pioneered the Al-Fin process, which utilized a chemical bond of aluminum to steel. This allowed airplane motors to be redesigned with different materials, which provided lighter-weight engines with improved cooling and added horsepower.[87] This allowed later models of the Hellcat F6F to have increased speed and achieve higher altitudes.

Since production quotas were being strictly enforced to keep up with demand, mistakes were common, and some were deadly. The most dangerous job in Grumman was that of the test pilot. Testing the planes came with a lengthy checklist, which included instrument tests, power ratings and balancing tests that were recorded to make adjustments.[88] Throughout the war, Grumman had five test pilots who were killed in flight; the most famous of them was Bobby McReynolds. On October 6, 1943, around 3:45 p.m., McReynolds was testing the Hellcats before they were shipped to the navy for military use. While flying one of the planes, it stalled out in midair and tumbled into the driveway of a house on Park Avenue in Farmingdale. The first responders who arrived at the scene of the crash found McReynolds crushed against the controls. The flaw of the crashed plane remained unclear and drew concern from the other four test pilots.

Three of the four remaining test pilots were women—Barbara Jayne, Elizabeth Hooker and one the media described as Mrs. Teddy Kenyon. Navigating planes that stalled out at thirty-five thousand feet and adjusting in midair and coasting close to four hundred miles per hour gave these test pilots indispensable skills. Jayne, who became distinguished in her ability to recover from nine-thousand-foot dives, went on to be the first female pilot instructor in Troy, New York. Her instruction trained not only civilian but

This page and opposite, top: The Navel Weapons Industrial Reserve Plant of Bethpage became Grumman's main production facility. It expanded to mass production in 1941. *Courtesy of the Library of Congress Photograph Catalog.*

A Bethpage Grumman–built Hellcat on an aircraft carrier in the Pacific. *Courtesy of the Library of Congress Photograph Catalog.*

also army and navy pilots. The quality checks and adjustments made by the test pilots to the planes before they were shipped made them more effective in the Pacific theater.

Until the close of the war, national media outlets praised the Hellcat's effectiveness as an individual hero of combat. "Grumman Hellcat, Navy's New Fighter Plane, Gets Baptism of Fire in Marcus Island Raid" was just one of the headlines that spanned across state and local papers on September 10, 1943. The article went on to say, "The plane became worthy of its name through its 350 individual strafing attacks, expending 150,000 rounds of .50-caliber ammunition."[89] Navy pilots showered the plane's handling, mobility and speed with praise, saying it could outmaneuver seasoned Japanese fighters. The plane's performance was further tested when it proved its ability to sink three Japanese destroyers. Headlines hailed it, saying, "Taking the fight to Chichi Island, which was 600 miles from Tokyo, sunk two destroyers and to southwest of the Marianas sunk a third."[90] These tests of endurance were just the beginning of the Hellcat's combat role.

United States Navy Air Group 12, under the command of Joseph Clinton, further pushed the limits of the Hellcats in combat. From September 1943, when Navy Air Group 12 adopted the Hellcat as its premier fighter, to late June 1944, the group destroyed 102 enemy planes, damaged 78, sunk 104,500 tons of enemy shipping and damaged an additional 198,500 tons.[91] In 1945, the group destroyed another 223 Japanese planes. This span of destruction within such a short time not only put Japan on the defensive but started to cripple its morale.

The success of this plane did not go unnoticed in Washington, D.C. In late June 1943, eight months after its introduction into combat, James Forrestal, the secretary of the navy, personally thanked the Bethpage Grumman plant for its production of the plane. In a statement telegrammed to plant manager Swirbul, he said, "Thank you for providing our aviators with the wings of victory."[92] Toward the end of the war, the navy researched ways to modify the Hellcat to make it even deadlier. The answer was the newly modified Ghost Hellcat, or Drone. The plane was wired to be radio-controlled and pilotless, making it the foundation of the modern-day drone. The navy experimented with packing the plane with explosives and using it as a radio-controlled missile.

Near the end of the war, the military's tactics shifted toward aviation combat. Destroying enemy supply lines became the key to ending the war. Fighter planes, such as the Hellcats, were great in defensive attacks and holding a front line, but the navy needed a torpedo bomber. The Hellcat

This page: Test pilots had the most dangerous jobs in aircraft manufacturing. Similar Hellcats, P-47 Thunderbolts had many flaws. Pictured is a P-47 covered in fire extinguishing foam between the houses of Eunice and Bernard Fixler and Mr. and Mrs. Walter R. Briggs near Mitchel Field. *Courtesy of the Hofstra University Library Special Collection.*

fighter plane was designed for one skilled fighter pilot, which made the task of shooting in defensive fire while trying to drop a torpedo tough. The TBF Avenger was designed to have a crew of three, which included a pilot, a gunner and a radio operator. The plane's armory included a fixed 7.62-millimeter gun by the nose of the plane on the right side, a 7.62-millimeter gun facing in the rear in a turret for a bombardier to operate and two M2 wing-mounted Browning machine guns. The plane had an additional capacity to hold and drop a 1,600-pound torpedo or bomb. Its top speed was 271 miles per hour with a range of 1,215 miles. A total of 9,835 Avengers were produced, and an estimated 2,000 were made by Grumman's plant in Bethpage. Unlike the Hellcat, the Avenger was used in the European theater as well as the Pacific theater. In the Atlantic, the Avenger became known for its depth in bombing Nazi U-boats, but the media did not hold the Avenger to the same standard and praise as the Hellcat.

As the Hellcat and Avenger's successful performances became well known, orders for the planes rolled in through the navy and American allies. With orders for the Avenger, the Wildcat and the Hellcat, Grumman in mid-1943 was backlogged until June 1945. To speed up its production, Grumman partnered with its would-be competitor Liberty Aircraft Corporation to make parts for the Hellcat. The construction of the Avenger also had to be split between Grumman and the General Motors Corporation to guarantee the on-time delivery of the planes for combat. Grumman's amphibian planes and other random aircraft parts were outsourced to Valley Stream's Columbia Aircraft Corporation. By 1944, despite outsourcing to competitors, Grumman produced more planes than any other plant in the country.[93] The planes with outsourced parts that were assembled by the Bethpage plant were the Grumman G-44 Widgeons, one of the few amphibian planes made there. Widgeons were used for U-boat surveillance, but similar to the Columbia XJL-1, the end of the war meant only three hundred were made.

Alexander Seversky founded Republic Aviation Corporation, which was originally named Seversky Aircraft Company. Seversky had a passion for aviation that was ingrained in him in the early years of aviation in Tsarist Russia. During World War I, Seversky served in the Russian Naval Fighter Fleet as a pilot and lost his leg in battle. This battle earned him a title in the Order of St. George for bravery in combat. After fleeing Russia during the Russian Revolution, Seversky went on to fulfill his passion in aviation by starting at Seversky Aircraft in 1923. His passion, unfortunately, did not carry over in bookkeeping, and the company had to reorganize in 1939, becoming Republic Aviation. The company's new modern manufacturing

Bethpage Grumman–made Avengers. They can be seen here flying in formation. *Courtesy of the Library of Congress Photograph Catalog.*

plant was constructed in Farmingdale, around the modern-day Republic Airport. The reorganization soon made the company a powerhouse in the industry. With the reorganization, Seversky's engineer, Alexander Kartvelishvili, became an asset. Under the direction of Kartvelishi, Republic pioneered the modern jet aircraft through his design of turbo jet fighters, such as P-43 Lancer, P-47 Thunderbolt, XP-72 and the postwar P-84B Thunder-Jet.[94] The innovative designs and speed of production became a force Grumman struggled to reckon with.

The Lancer P-43 was the framework for Republic's first successful turbojet. The single-seat P-43 was originally produced in 1940 and 1941, and it was ordered by the Australian and Chinese defense forces. The plane was powered by the innovative Pratt & Whitney 1830–49 1,200 horsepower motor, which took the P-43 to a top speed of 357 miles per hour, with an altitude limit of 36,000 feet and a range of 650 miles. The production of this plane was disrupted by the reorganization of Seversky to Republic, which kept the total number of produced planes at 272. The largest success of the Lancer was the foundation it created for future turbojets.

One of the greatest planes from World War II, aside from the Hellcat, was the 1942 P-47 Thunderbolt. Similar to the Hellcat, the media and the Long Island community rallied behind this fighter plane with pride as if it was a legendary war hero from a small town. Francis "Gabby" Gabreski, who later made Dix Hills his home, was a flight leader in the Sixty-First Fighter Squadron. Known for his success in combating Nazi air fights, he used to mark his fighter planes with a Nazi symbol for each Nazi plane he took out. After becoming a media sensation, all his pictures were taken next to his P-47 Thunderbolt. In interviews, he credited his P-47's handling with his victories. On July 5, 1944, he became the top flying ace in the war, outpacing all of the previous records with a total of twenty-eight downed Nazi planes. Following his record-setting conquests, Gabreski was promoted to the rank of lieutenant colonel. His grit may have led him to have a high success rate, but his ability to outflank any Nazi plane in the Luftwaffe made his P-47 a legend of American engineering in combat.

Cousin to the P-43 Lancer, the P-47 single-seat plane had features that included a 2,300 horsepower Pratt & Whitney engine, six to eight fifty-caliber machine guns, an armor-plated cockpit and self-sealing fuel tanks that protected the plane from punctures. The craft had a range of 1,000 miles, the ability to carry a 2,500-pound bomb, a top speed of over 428 miles per hour and an altitude limit of 42,000 feet. The German Luftwaffe could not come close to competing with its performance. Unlike the $35,000 price point of the Hellcat, the Thunderbolt cost $83,000 per plane. This plane was exclusively used in the European theatre. The British Royal Navy, French Fighter and Soviet Union Fighter Fleet used a total of seven hundred Thunderbolts to fight the German advances under America's Lend-Lease Program.

This page: Laborers working on the predecessor to the Republic P-43 Lancer, the P-47 Thunderbolt. *Courtesy of the Library of Congress Photograph Catalog.*

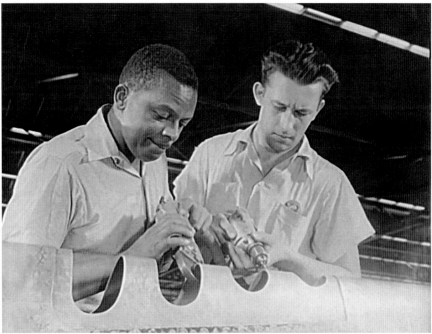

The most famous distinction the P-47 had outside of battle was its effective production process. In total, more than 15,579 P-47s were made, which set the record for the highest production of a single plane model in American history. In less than two years, Republic was able to fill an order of 6,500 planes, which were all expected for a two-and-a-half-year delivery.

This page: Republic workers installing the propeller of the P-47 Thunderbolt. *Courtesy of the Library of Congress Photograph Catalog.*

Francis Gabreski in the cockpit of his P-47 Thunderbolt, showing off his new record of downing twenty-eight Nazi planes. He credited his P-47 with the success. *Courtesy of the National Achieves World War II Collection.*

Amazed by the speed and quality of Republic's production, Lieutenant Colonel Thomas Murphy, who represented the Federal Department of War, came to Republic to congratulate the workers on jobs well done. Among the crowds of employees, people were heard bragging, "Hitler's going to get his belly full now, thanks to our planes."[95] The company's success was due to management being obsessed with the average manhours it took to produce one Thunderbolt. When production first began for the Thunderbolt, the average manhours it took to construct one plane was 22,927, but by 1944, the company set (and achieved) a goal to get this number down to 7,729.[96] With the reduction in manhours, the price of the plane dropped from $83,000 to $68,000.

In September 1944, Republic outproduced all of the other aviation manufacturing companies of single-seat fighter planes in the nation when the ten thousandth Thunderbolt rolled off the production line in Farmingdale. In early 1945, the company surpassed all expectations by getting the plane's construction time down to 6,290 manhours, and it reduced the price of the plane to $45,600, which was still in competition with Grumman's $35,000 Hellcat. The total cost savings with the reduced manhours saved Republic $100 million. And these savings were passed on in the form of more contracts with the war department. The plane became so widespread in American combat that two out of every three fighter pilots flew a Thunderbolt in combat.

Republic not only manufactured turbojets for the military, it also got into the manufacturing of bombs that were utilized in the European theater. To keep up with the design and cutting-edge engineering of bombs, Republic had to first replicate what the Germans had. This opportunity arose on June

Mitchel Field with a newly delivered Republic P-47 in its first hangar. The P-47 became the most mass-produced fighter plane in military history. All 15,579 were made in the Republic Farmingdale plant. *Courtesy of the Cradle of Aviation Museum of Nassau County Image Collection.*

13, 1944, the bloodiest day of the war in London. Starting on June 13, 1944, and lasting until March 27, 1945, London was struck by hundreds of V1 bombs. These bombs were the predecessors of the modern-day cruise missiles, and they operated on a radio-control guidance system that was powered by a small engine. In the first eighty days of the V1 attacks, an estimated six thousand civilians were killed, with only 33 percent—and later 9 percent—of the bombs breaking through the English defensive lines. With several of these bombs littered across London, various defense contractors wanted one to study in an effort to replicate them.

The V1 and V2 Nazi bombs could reach an airspeed of 400 miles per hour and had a range of 250 miles. In 1944, Republic became the first manufacturer to win a contract to produce these early cruise missiles. Republic won this contract due to its speed in filling prior contracts, not its cheaper price point. Once it won the contract, a German V1 was shipped to the Farmingdale facility to be taken apart and replicated by engineers. Similar to the V1, the Republic JB-2 made a buzzing sound as it approached its target, so military servicemen nicknamed them buzz bombs. The JB-2 could travel at 425 miles per hour and had a range of 150 miles. Similar to the V1, these bombs were radio controlled, but they were powered by a Ford pulse jet motor. Throughout the war, Republic produced a total of 1,391 JB-2s. Motors for the JB-2 were constructed by Ford and later installed in the bombs. The total cost of the production of these bombs was estimated to be $3,000 per unit. The first set of bombs that were shipped out from Farmingdale to Newark Army Airfield had personalized messages written in chalk that read, "A kiss for Hitler."[97]

A Republic JB-2 Buzz Bomb: over one thousand were produced in the Farmingdale Republic plant. *Courtesy of the Cradle of Aviation Museum of Nassau County Image Collection.*

Once in combat, these bombs were used toward the end of the war in Europe and in the Pacific theater.

The planes and bombs produced by Long Island manufacturers and their over 100,000 workers were some of the factors that paved the way for an American victory. The collective efforts of the community to mobilize a workforce that made up less than half the population of Nassau and Suffolk Counties and to produce effective and streamlined aircraft manufacturing trade programs were in themselves amazing achievements. Salvage drives and bond-buying campaigns not only raised needed resources for the war but also democratized the war effort for everyone. Becoming an active participant in the war, in effect, made one a stakeholder and a part of the shared vision of achieving victory.

7.

POWs OFF AND ON LONG ISLAND

As the war progressed, American soldiers on the European and Pacific fronts captured more and more prisoners of war (POWs). Toward the end of the war, 425,871 German, Italian and Japanese prisoners were shipped to temporary detention camps in various parts of the United States. Once they were brought to America, the U.S. military command stressed the humanitarian treatment of all detainees. Most of the camps were open dorms with access to local communities, and prisoners were assigned to do work, such as farm labor.

On Long Island, the three main places where POWs were held were Mason General Hospital in Brentwood/Deer Park, Camp Upton in Brookhaven and Mitchel Field in Hempstead. Upton had an estimated 1,500 POWs, and Mitchel Field had an estimated 300 POWs throughout the war. The record of the number of POWs held in Mason General for long-term detention—or throughout the duration of the war—has been lost to history. All the POWs held on Long Island were between the ages of sixteen and fifty years old. When shipped to Long Island, the POWs suffered from various physical and mental health problems. Being captured in long bloody battles brought not only the challenges of trauma but also malnutrition and various diseases. A total of 89 POWs died while in detention at Camp Upton, Mason General Hospital and Mitchel Field. These soldiers were interred in Long Island National Cemetery, which is present-day Pinelawn Cemetery in Farmingdale.

Mason General Hospital, later renamed Edgewood, was constructed in the late 1930s with Federal Works Progress Administration (WPA) grants. Originally planned as an extension for Pilgrim Psychiatric Hospital, Edgewood became another depot to house the area's growing number of psychiatric patients. Located in the Oak Brush Plains area of Western Suffolk County, the campus of Pilgrim and the proposed extension would have comprised over 3,000 acres. The seclusion of the area and the fact that the hospital had its own railroad stop made it an ideal location for the military. In 1943, the military, under the leadership of Colonel Robert B. Hill, issued General Order 59, which took over the Edgewood Hospital and the 938 acres surrounding the facility. The facility, under military ownership, was renamed Mason General Hospital. The hospital was named in honor General Charles Field Mason, who was known for his work on combating yellow fever epidemics during the American campaign in the Philippines and the construction of Panama Canal. The military originally leased the facility for training in neuropsychiatry for the medical corps under Colonel William C. Porter. In total, the facility had 2,621 beds to assist those who had sustained emotional trauma in the war.

In 1944, following the lease of the land and the progression of war operations in Europe and the Pacific, the United States military extended the hospital into Pilgrim Buildings 81, 82, and 60. In a departure from the military's original goal of making Mason General Hospital a training facility for the medical corps, the hospital's operations extended to include a tuberculosis ward and a POW camp. Soldiers diagnosed with "combat fatigue," later defined as post-traumatic stress syndrome, were treated with electric shock therapy, sodium amytal and music therapy. Many of the POWs held at the hospital were considered high-risk due to their mental states, high enemy ranking or suspected homosexual tendencies.[98] Once they were isolated from the other POW camps, the captured soldiers were secured in locked rooms with limited recreation time in monitored dayrooms. As compared to the open dorm set up of the other camps, Mason General had a restrictive environment.

Around 8:15 p.m. on November 8, 1946, the war was over, and the POWs were slowly being shipped back to their countries of origin. With the close of the war, POWs were still kept under restrictive status, as they were still considered security risks. Four men, three American soldiers from the Black regiments who were being court-martialed after being declared "unmanageable" and a high-risk Nazi POW who had been declared psychopathic, led a mix of twelve additional POWs and American soldiers who were awaiting court-martial into a battle with two hundred military police. The men, armed with makeshift clubs made from wooden benches, took on the guards from the dayroom on the seventh floor to the exit, which gave three of the men the opportunity to steal a car and escape.[99] The fourth man, George Wilson, hid out in the dense forest that surrounded the hospital, but he was caught eleven hours later by Pilgrim State Hospital authorities. The other three men, including the Nazi, abandoned the car in Bay Shore's downtown, by Park Avenue. By hiding out in an ally loading dock at Bohack's Store on Main Street, the trio managed to dodge authorities until 3:30 a.m. Since they were wearing nothing but the hospital-issued pajamas to protect them from the cold, a concerned local called the state troopers to report suspicious men lurking around stores after hours. State troopers George Lake and William Brockman took the trio by surprise, and without a struggle, they were returned to Mason General. Despite this bold escape, there was no other recorded revolts or escape attempts.

Camp Upton, located in Brookhaven Suffolk County, was located in the Pine Barren region. The camp, established during World War I, comprised over nine thousand acres. The camp transitioned metropolitan inductees into army units, and it served as a waiting area until overseas assignments were issued. On September 1, 1944, army officials announced that the camp would suspend its operations as a reception area for army inductees. The camp was then broken up into sections for a rehabilitation center and a detention center for AWOL soldiers, other fractious military members and war threats.[100] What was not disclosed to the public was that it was going to be utilized for foreign POWs and that it had to undergo a costly renovation.

With the predicted number of POWs in dire physical and mental health sent to the camp growing, Upton opened a temporary 3,500-bed hospital and open dorm. The new construction was partially used as a method to model the success of a democratic society, and it had every luxury possible. The facility had seventy-one barrack buildings, which included state-of-the art medical technology, a dental wing, a dayroom, a library, an indoor therapeutic swimming pool, a remedial gym, a bowling alley and a music studio. The dorm had an open floor plan that allowed for the least restrictive movement within the camp; prisoners there even had access to the hospital and other facilities without escorts. The housing facilities for the prisoners were wood structures that had canvases stretched over them and a small coal stove. Five POWs were assigned to each structure. In an effort to model the fair practices of capitalism, POWs were given jobs on the base and were paid the current market wage of eighty cents

This page: Mason General Hospital, which was later renamed Edgewood, was located in the Oak Brush Plains area of Western Suffolk County. Originally planned as an extension for Pilgrim Psychiatric Hospital, Mason General housed the highest-profile and most dangerous POWS. *Courtesy of the Library of Congress Photograph Catalog.*

per day. Working POWs were paid in the form of coupons, which they were allowed to use as currency in the local canteen or store. The dorms included a school for the prisoners; there, they were taught academics with a reeducation program to combat the indoctrination of Nazism. Once they completed the reeducation program, detainees were sent back home to their countries of origin.

The camp's first group of foreign prisoners (not counting the domestic internment of the 148 New York residents born in Japan, Germany and Italy) were the forty-five crew members of the German ship *Odenwald*. This German merchant ship was a blockade runner and was stocked with tires and other equipment for the German army. In November 1941, the United States Navy was experimenting with bounties on captured blockade runners, and the crew of the USS *Omaha* was determined to earn its first $34,000 bonus.

On November 6, the navy came across a boat that claimed it come from the Port of Philadelphia in the south Atlantic. Following an examination of the boat's paperwork, it was discovered that it was a German merchant ship. The crew was shipped to Upton, and the goods of the boat were auctioned off. That same year, three Italians, and twenty-three Germans from Colombia and Saint Lucia were suspected of participating in international espionage. A Swiss legation was put in charge of the German and Italian POWs, and they were to report back on whether or not they had fair treatment as prisoners and if America was abiding by the Genova Treaty. In a report, the Swiss legation said that the camp had made a much better impression on him than he had expected, and after interviewing several of the detainees, it was found that bland food was the main complaint.[101] Other complaints included that the captain of the *Odenwald* shared a cabin with people below his rank and that the visit time for domestic internees was too brief. Internee Hein Berthing stated that he and others were only allowed to see their wives once a week for fifteen minutes, and they demanded the time be extended. Building on the visitation complaint, Hein further argued that the welfare of his family was in jeopardy due to his inability to earn a wage to send back to them.

This small number of war detainees did not draw concern from locals, and during the years between 1941 and 1944, Upton had an overwhelming number of soldiers in training. The community took notice in April 1945, when the first shipment of five hundred German and Italian POWs arrived. Prior to the arrival of these POWs, the domestic internees were shipped out to Camp Meade Maryland. These prisoners arrived surprised at the

Opposite and above: The modified Camp Upton, pictured here, was meant to secure the growing number of POWs coming into to America. *Courtesy of the Longwood Library, Bayles Local History Room and Photograph Archives.*

Left: The most famous guard of the POW camp at Upton was famous boxer Joe Lewis. *Courtesy of the Library of Congress Photograph Catalog.*

amenities and resources available to them. In a letter from a former Upton POW, dated July 12, 1946, Josef Kraft, who befriended Upton civilian worker Pearsall, stated:

> *I am often thinking about the good times in the Besches Mess in Camp Upton. Here, in Germany, we have to do without quite a lot, which wasn't the case over there. Most often, I am thinking of the good food and the smoking, which we had when I was together with you in the dining hall.…Should you still be working in the dining hall, please give my best regards to all who knew me, in particular, to the German women who worked in the dining hall.*[102]

This comparison between what Germany had and what the POW camp had was supposed to have displayed the failures of Nazism and the success of American democracy.

While enjoying the state-of-the-art medical facilities and educational programs, prisoners had the ability to apply for paying jobs on the base. Due to complaints about domestic detainees being unable to provide for their families, the base agreed to a higher pay that almost matched civilian workers. Unlike the POW camp at Mitchel Field in Nassau County, Upton was surrounded by the county's largest farms, which limited the employment opportunities there for locals. Many locals viewed jobs at Camp Upton as ways to earn a livable wage; one such job was that of a truck driver. Following the influx of prisoners to the camp in 1945, POWs were put to work as truck drivers, and Albert Goll, the commander of the Sayville American Legion, took notice. In a formal complaint, Goll said the POWs were only authorized by the federal government to do farmwork, as there was a shortage, and that truck drivers were never authorized, as that was usually a job reserved for American veterans.[103]

Once this letter became public, locals started to criticize the treatment of POWs in the camp. In the opinions of many locals, the detainees were receiving better medical care, dental care and educational programs than they were. Local papers stated, "Mitchel Field and Camp Upton have coddled enemy prisoners at the expense of American wounded soldiers and even chastised them with a slap on the wrists."[104] These headlines led to rumors of riots from POWs demanding more beer with their dinner, which created more local outrage. This rumor of extra beer came at a time when many Americans could not afford a beer with their dinner, as rationed food in the markets was still a reality.

Anton-Günther-Schule

Staatliche Oberschule für Jungen

Annaberg i. Erzgeb.

Abgangs-Zeugnis.

Paul Emil Herbert S c h ö n h e r r

geboren zu Schlettau i. Erzgeb.   am 13. Juli   1925

Sohn des Kaufmanns Herbert S c h ö n h e r r

wurde am 15. April   1936 in die Klasse VI(1) der Anton-Günther-Schule

zu Annaberg i. Erzgeb., Staatliche Oberschule für Jungen, aufgenommen und verläßt die

Anstalt am 15. Mai   19 43 aus Klasse 8. Beim Abgang sind ihm

folgende Zensuren erteilt worden:

Allgemeine Beurteilung:

Schönherr ist in den Leibesübungen einsatzbereit.Seine Leistungen

in den Wissenschaften und Künsten entsprechen seinen Anlagen.und

seinem Fleiß.

Fachzensuren:

Deutsch	2	Physik	3
Geschichte	2	Rechnen und Mathematik	4
Erdkunde	2	Englisch	4
Kunsterziehung	2	Latein	3
Musik	3	Religionslehre	
Biologie	2	Französische Arbeitsgemeinschaft	—
Chemie	4		

Bemerkungen:

Dem Schüler wird auf Grund der nachgewiesenen Einberufung zum
Wehrdienst gemäß Erlaß des Herrn Reichsministers für Wissenschaft,
Erziehung und Volksbildung vom 8. September 1939 - E III a Nr.1947,
W, RV (b) - die Reife zuerkannt.

Annaberg i. Erzgeb.,

am 15. Mai   19 43

(Schulstempel)   Oberstudiendirektor

Bedeutung der Ziffern:

1 = sehr gut, 2 = gut, 3 = befriedigend, 4 = ausreichend, 5 = mangelhaft, 6 = ungenügend.

This paperwork about the rank of Nazi soldiers was found on a POW being processed at Camp Upton. *Courtesy of the Longwood Library, Bayles Local History Room and Photograph Archives.*

ARMY SERVICE FORCES
Second Service Command
1234th SCU PW Camp
Camp Upton   New York

31 March 1946

I certify that Prisoner of War S C H O E N H E R R , PAUL
ISN 31G 12 000   was received at the 1234th SCU PW Camp,
Camp Upton, N.Y. as a "Detained Prisoner of War". During the time
he has been under our jurisdiction his work and behaviour has been
very satisfactory or better. Although he was classified as "Detained"
pursuant to instructions received from higher authority, his actions
and attitude while here have been in direct contradiction to the
teachings and doctrine of the Nazi party. His performance of duty
and his attitude have been such as to win the approbation and respect
of the American personnel of this camp and the personnel under whom
he worked.
        He has shown a great interest in the classes conducted by our
Intellectual Diversion Section for the re-orientation of the German
Prisoners of War to the "American Way" of living.
        It is my firm conviction that, as a result of the classes in
which he participated, and as a result of the close contact with the
PW staff and other American personnel, he has acquired a favorable
attitude toward "American ideology"; and as a civilian will be a
decided asset to the United Nations in any re-orientation program
we may undertake for Germany.

A.L.HAGGE
Lt.Col CAC
Comdg.

Above and opposite, top: A behavior recommendation report and personal reference for
German POW Paul Schoenherr, who was held at Camp Upton on March 1946. *Courtesy of
the Longwood Library, Bayles Local History Room and Photograph Archives.*

Opposite, bottom: Paul Schoenherr's certificate of completion for a deradicalization program.
This program taught POWs the American values of democracy and the English language.
Courtesy of the Longwood Library, Bayles Local History Room and Photograph Archives.

ARMY SERVICE FORCES
SECOND SERVICE COMMAND
1234th SCU PW CAMP
CAMP UPTON, NEW YORK

201 - Schoenherr, Paul   10 April 1946

C E R T I F I C A T E

To Whom It May Concern:

    I certify that PW Paul SCHOENHERR, 31 G 12000, has been a member
of the 1234th SCU PW Camp, Camp Upton, N. Y., since 20 November 1945.
Throughout his stay at this camp he has been very cooperative, and has
been an excellent worker. He gave active support to the intellectual
diversion program at this camp, first as a student, and later as an
instructor in English. He is favorably disposed toward American
Ideology.

A. L. HAGGART
Lt Col   CAC
Commanding

PRISONER OF WAR CAMP
CAMP UPTON, LONG ISLAND

This **certificate of achievement** is awarded to

Paul Schoenherr

who has succesfully completed a course in   English conversation

for Prisoners of War conducted at CAMP UPTON, New York.

In witness thereof, the undersigned have hereunto set their names this
_____ day of April 10. 1946.

Edwin L. Dooley
1st Lt., CMP   Ass't Executive Officer

Wilhelm Fischer
Wilhelm Fischer
PW Director of Studies

A. L. HAGGART
Lt. Col., CAC   PW Camp Commander

Since POWs were authorized to do farm labor, the Long Island Farm Institute petitioned the government to get the POWs to work on the farms in an effort alleviate the labor shortage of field hands. Nassau and Suffolk Counties, in working with the War Food Administration, could not come to an agreement on the amount of additional labor needed for the potato season. Despite the pleas from the farmers, reports written by Albert Mather, the head of the Agricultural Adjustment Agency, used average crop yields from prior years and said, "Suffolk County is not suffering from a manpower shortage, due to the estimated 500 Jamaican migrant workers that were sent to the island for this season."[105] This report underestimated the crop size for the 1945 season and the bad weather that limited laborers from digging up potatoes.

POWs were desirable laborers because they were at peak health and had good discipline. Long Island growers, in the 1945 season, were receiving nine cents per bushel of potatoes, as compared to the season prior when they received six cents. Farmers estimated that an able-bodied man could dig up two hundred bushels a day, which allowed worker to earn eighteen dollars a day. In a letter to New York senator Robert Wagner, John Froehlich, the president of the Long Island Farm Institute said that the federal estimation on labor was low and, "without the war prisoners to dig the potatoes, [they] would probably not get the required crop results by Christmas."[106]

Camp Upton at its peak population, before its prisoners were assigned to harvest potato crops for local farmers. *Courtesy of the Longwood Library, Bayles Local History Room and Photograph Archives.*

Wagner's failure to promptly respond got local congressman Leonard Hall to petition General Thomas Terry, the commanding officer of the Second Service Command that over saw POW operations in New York, for the needed labor. Hall, representing Suffolk and Nassau Counties advocated for the POWs of not only Upton but also Mitchel Field to work on potato farms in both counties. With the congressional pressure, 420 POWs from Upton were sent to work on fifty thousand acres of Suffolk County potato farms. In Nassau County, 45 of the Mitchel Field POWs were ordered to work the county's farms. The difference in numbers was due to Mitchel Field having a smaller POW population, as the base still fully operational for day-to-day military operations. The pay for the POWs was fixed at eighty cents a day, and workers were divided between the potato silo and the potato field. Mitchel Field and Upton commanders promised tight security when the prisoners were escorted to the farms, but this security became relaxed following the first season. At Mitchel Field, some of the local farmers, such as Joseph Rhodes of Marcus Avenue, Garden City, would pick up the German POWs themselves, every morning at 5:30 a.m., without any security detail.

The treatment of POWs on Long Island reflected the strengths of American society, especially when put into contrast with the treatment of American soldiers in German POW camps, where the treatment was inhumane. One American POW was Huntington resident Sergeant Michael Colamonico of the Air Force's 327th Bomb Squadron. Colamonico was captured on December 31, 1943, by the Germans while working the turret gun on a B-17 bomber over France. Four Americans, including Colamonico, were sent to a Gestapo interrogation center in Frankfurt. While there, Colamonico was kept in extreme isolation for nine days, which is when he forced himself to

come to terms with his mortality. While praying in isolation, Colamonico claimed to have a vision of Christ confronting him.[107] After unsuccessful interrogation attempts in which Nazi officials found out he had no intel, Colamonico was shipped off to Camp Stalag 17 in Austria.

From Frankfurt, Colamonico was put into a crowded box car with standing room only, something he described as coming from the movie *Schindler's List*.[108] Once Colamonico arrived at the camp, his head was shaved, and he was assigned to stay in a garage-like building. He said the cold in the building was so intense that people had to huddle together in an effort to not freeze to death. The only meals Colamonico received were pieces of bread made from sawdust and a little grain and half a cup of coffee to wash them down. While in the camp, the treatment he received was described as brutal, but when SS commanders visited the camp, treatment became even worse. In interviews, Colamonico was hesitant to describe the physical and emotional treatment he received there, citing that it made him uncomfortable to talk about it again. After Colamonico endured eighteen months of abuse, the camp was liberated by American troops on May 3, 1945.

Some POWs received even worse treatment, such as William Marcario of Bayville and Walter Lutkiewiez of Westbury. When taken into custody, Marcario was taken to a Gestapo office, where he had to kneel down with his hands, which were tied under his knees, for hours of interrogation. Lutkiewiez was taken to labor camp, were he saw dozens of workers die from pure exhaustion.

In some German POW camps, the Red Cross became the only source of food for American POWs. Following his release, American POW Major Raymond Sanford of the United States Air Corps, who was stationed at Mitchel Field in Nassau County, detailed the dire treatment in prison camps. After his B-17 was shot down over Amsterdam on December 13, 1943, he was shipped to Stalag Luff 1. Once he arrived, he noticed the camp was overfilled with over ten thousand people who looked like walking skeletons. When the war took a bad turn for the Nazis, they stopped feeding the prisoners and refused any Red Cross parcels that were sent to assist in feeding them. When Sanford was near death due to starvation, the Nazis agreed to feed the POWs, but only with food provided by the Red Cross. This decision was made because delegates from Geneva, Switzerland, were coming to inspect the camps to see if they complied with the Geneva Convention. The delegation gave them notice months in advance, which gave the Nazis time to present a different reality. After losing forty pounds, Sanford credited his survival with the Red Cross parcels, which not only fed the prisoners but also gave them hope.[109] Stanford's experience was in the headlines of every newspaper; it was used to highlight the importance of the Red Cross and the treatment of Americans who were at the mercy of the Germans.

The Red Cross not only supplied the POWs with food but also even helped bring injured POWs home when Germans persisted in holding them. Army private Bernie Rader of Freeport, during his first deployment, was captured with fifty-five other Americans in France. Rader's capture followed a six-hour firefight, planned to repel a German ambush of an American army unit. Wounded from shrapnel in both his legs and arms, Rader had no other option but to surrender to the mercy of the Nazi forces. Realizing his dog tags identified him as Jewish, Rader asked fellow soldier private George Boyd to bury his tags in a ditch before his surrender. With his one good arm, Boyd dragged himself to Rader, ripped his tags off and buried them. He said in a joking matter, "I buried your identity and religion all in the same hole."[110] Nazi forces surrounded the area and transported Rader and the other injured American soldiers to an old captured French medical unit.

While at the medical unit, Rader stated he was not treated the same as someone in a prison camp, but he said there was no anesthesia, morphine or hydrochloride, which made the screams of injured solders echo through the entire unit. For food, they were given two slices of bread with one cup of soup a day. Rader and the other 148 men in the medical unit were near starvation until a Red Cross volunteer named Andrew Hodge brought food and needed medical supplies to them. While in the unit Hodge came to understand that the situation of the 149 wounded soldiers was dire, and he tried to work out a negation their release to a proper facility. Following a forty-seven-day stay, Hodge got Rader and the other 148 soldiers released in a prisoner exchange agreement.

As the war reached its peak, communication with captured soldiers broke down. Many soldiers were being classified as missing in action (MIA) or assumed killed in action (KIA). One Patchogue resident named Irene Walter, a mother herself, empathized with other mothers who did not know the fate of their sons on the combat lines. While everyone was asleep in her home on one evening in 1942, Irene was getting to know how to work a shortwave radio. To her surprise, she was able to pick up a Nazi propaganda broadcast, which American military officials referred to as "Axis Sally." During the Axis Sally broadcasts, a list of captured and wounded American soldier's addresses, serial numbers and names was read in an effort to display the progress of the Nazi war machine. Realizing the importance of this information, Irene recorded it. Soon, this became an at-home job for Irene. She described her daily routine:

> *I would write postcards to all address provided with the updates of the soldiers, and sometimes, I would be up until 3 or 4 a.m. I would never put down what was wrong with the boys if they were hospitalized—just they were alive. The following day, I would have my son drop off all the postcards to the post office on his way to school.*[111]

One concerned parent was even able to locate the prison camp their soldier was in based on the broadcasts Irene recorded. Irene continued her work until the end of the war and received thousands of responses that either inquired about more on the status of their loved one or expressed their appreciation.

By mid-1946, the German POWs in Long Island were shipped back to occupied Germany. Mitchel Field shipped its last 233 Germans back to Germany on March 22. When the German POWs were shipped back, the media described them as Hitler's henchmen, who scoffed at the accounts of Nazi brutalities at Dachau, Bergen-Belsen and Buchenwald, as their personal treatment in America was far above the Geneva Convention standards.[112] The headlines of German brutality added to the locals' anger, but the good-paying jobs the POWs got on the local bases for eighty cents a day—above the average pay of many Long Islanders—turned the anger on military officials. The public, outraged that the Nazis were not treated as criminals, overlooked the successful work done by these camps in the deradicalization of the prisoners' Nazi ideology.

8

MEDAL OF HONOR RECIPIENTS OF LONG ISLAND

The Congressional Medal of Honor is the highest recognition a soldier can receive for their conduct in battle. The process of being nominated is lengthy and starts with a submission to the Department of the Army, Navy, Air Force, or Marine Human Resource Command. Then, the recommendation goes to the decoration board for a review of its merit, and then to the secretary of defense, who either approves or disapproves. The final approval is given by the president, who also formally awards the medal. Throughout World War II, 460 Medals of Honor were given out. From the 460, only 198 were given out to soldiers who did not die in combat. Two Long Islanders received the medal following their deaths in World War II, and three were awarded the medal after being demobilized. Throughout Long Island, blocks, roads, parks and overpasses are named after these five men.

Anthony Casamento from West Islip signed up to join the marines on August 19, 1940. Following the attack on Pearl Harbor, Casamento was deployed to the Pacific. The Campaign of Guadalcanal, also referred to as Operation Watchtower, was fought from August 7, 1942, to February 1943 on the British Soloman Islands. The fighting was nothing short of a baptism of blood. On November 1, land actions were in full swing following naval attacks. Along the Matanikau River, Company D, First Battalion, Fifth Marines was under heavy fire from Japanese forces. Machine gun leader Corporal Casamento had his unit advance along a ridge to provide cover fire for other units. While manning his machine gun, Casamento's entire unit was either killed or critically wounded. Despite this, and almost certain of his death Casamento, held his ground and secured the flank for other companies, all while being seriously wounded and falling in and out of consciousness.[113]

Casamento was later relieved of duty, as he was in critical condition from the serval wounds he received in the battle. Defeating the odds, Casamento lived, and thirty-eight years after his demonstration of valor, on September 12, 1980, he was awarded the Medal of Honor by President Jimmy Carter. Seven years later, at the age of sixty-six, Casamento died from cancer at the Northport VA. But his legacy is honored locally in the communities of West Islip and Bay Shore. Popular Casamento Park was named in his honor, and on the way to Casamento Park, visitors drive over Casamento Memorial Bridge. Five minutes west, Route 109 in Babylon was renamed Casamento Highway to further encapsulate his legacy.

Charles Shea was born in the Bronx, and as a high school graduate, he sold peanuts and soda at Yankee Stadium. From this job, he started exploring a career as a refrigeration mechanic. The year after the attack on Pearl Harbor, Charles signed up for the United States Army. He became part of the 350th Infantry of the 88th Division, Company F, and he rose to the rank of sergeant. His unit was assigned to the European theater. While on deployment in Italy, near Mount Damiano outside of Cassino, in May 1944, his company came under attack from heavy artillery. Following thirty causalities in his unit, Shea ran down the center line, gripping his rifle and grenades, toward the Nazi machine gun nests. Outrunning enemy fire and dodging bullets—in an almost unimaginable way—Shea took out three machine gun nests, one by one, singlehandedly. In total, his actions killed three German gunners and captured six German soldiers, which allowed his unit to advance toward Rome.

Charles Shea was promoted to the rank of lieutenant colonel and received a nomination for the Medal of Honor from General Mark Clark. After the war, he settled in Plainview Nassau County, but he was not be able to stay away from public service following his honorable discharge. In civilian life, Shea enlisted in the national guard (First Battalion, Sixty-Ninth Infantry New York) from 1949 to 1972. On April 7, 1994, Shea died of a heart attack in his home at the age of seventy-two.

Joseph Schaefer of Richmond Hill first enlisted in the United States Army in 1937 and received an honorable discharge eight months before the attack on Peral Harbor. With the headlines of the devastation suffered at Pearl Harbor, Schaefer reenlisted in the army, and for the second time, he was shipped to Camp Upton in Yaphank. Once he arrived in Upton, Schaefer got his deployment orders for the Eighteenth Infantry Regiment, First Infantry Division, in the European theater. While in Stolberg, Germany, on September 24, 1944, his platoon was ambushed by Nazi companies. Part of his platoon was captured, and Schaefer, left holding the position with a handful of other men, was greatly outnumbered. After running into a vacant building, they tried to come up with a plan to regroup the shattered platoon, and Schaefer, with his M1 Grand and some grenades, volunteered to take up a position that was seen as suicidal. Alone, Schaefer ran straight into the frontline, with little to no cover, to take out heavily armed Germans with flamethrowers. Schaefer continued to hold his position through rapid fire on a second wave of German attacks. In this firefight, Shaefer killed an estimated twelve Nazi troops, forcing the advancing troops to retreat. While advancing, he took up a position at the head of another platoon and liberated the American squad that had been captured earlier in the day.[114] His actions earned him the Medal of Honor on August 22, 1945. Shaefer continued his military career in the Korean War. On March 16, 1987, Schaefer died at the age of sixty-eight and was buried in Pine Lawn in Farmingdale.

One of the key attributes to being awarded the Medal of Honor is self-sacrifice. Bernard James Ray of Baldwin, Nassau County, was raised to serve his community. Ray, a member and, later, leader of Boy Scout Troop 126, recited the Boy Scout Oath at the beginning of every meeting. The first lines of the oath are, "On my honor, I will do my best to do my duty to God and my country." He lived by this oath from his preadolescence to the day he died at the age of twenty-three in the Hurtgen Forest in Germany, November 17, 1944. At the outbreak of World War II, Ray signed up for the United States Army, and he eventually rose to the rank of lieutenant. He was later assigned as a platoon leader to Company F, Eighth Infantry. While on a patrol in the Hurtgen Forrest, his company came under attack and was blocked in by a wire barricade and a landmine path. To free his men from the advancing Germans, Ray knew the barricade had to be blown up. So, with no regard for his own safety, Ray ran toward the barricade with a blasting cap and explosive primer cord in an effort to take out the obstacle. While on this dangerous mission, Ray was wounded by a barrage of mortar fire. In a gallant decision, Ray hastily wired together his ammunition, his body wrapped in the wire, and pushed the charger plunger.[115]

On December 8, 1945, Ray was awarded the Medal of Honor. On October 28, 1947, Bernard Ray came home. His body was transported from Germany to Pine Lawn Cemetery in East Farmingdale. Landing in Mitchel

Field, his homecoming was celebrated in Baldwin by the 581st Army Air Corps Band and a three-division parade to Long Island Station Plaza, where a monument and dedication service was conducted in the park that had recently been renamed in Ray's honor. Adding to the homecoming honor, thirty-five army air corps planes flew in a circle above the park in a show of solidarity. But the most impactful guest at this celebration was Ray's old Boy Scout Troop 126, whose members stood at attention with full understanding of duty to God and country.

Bravery and courage can sometimes be hereditary, especially when your last name is Roosevelt. Theodore Roosevelt Jr. carried the name and legacy of his father, the twenty-sixth president and war hero of San Juan Hill. Ten years his junior, Roosevelt Jr.'s brother Quentin distinguished himself in battle during World War I and died in combat near Normandy, France. His sacrifice became immortalized throughout his hometown of Oyster Bay, where Roosevelt Field was named in honor of his bravery. During World War I, Roosevelt Jr. served but did not distinguish himself as much as his younger brother. When World War II broke out, Theodore Roosevelt Jr. took a break from his political and business career as the governor of Puerto Rico and the Philippines and president of Doubleday Publishing to take military refresher courses.

Following his reenlistment into the United States Army, Roosevelt Jr. was promoted to brigadier general and was assigned command over Twenty-Sixth Infantry Regiment. Following his success in the North African Campaign in Algeria, the planning of the D-Day invasion was underway. The storming of Normandy held strong significance for Roosevelt Jr., as his son Quentin II was picked to serve in the invasion, and Normandy was the place where his younger brother died during World War I. Hiding his increasing heart problems and arthritis, Roosevelt Jr. demanded to command the Fourth Infantry, which was going to be the first wave of invading troops. Once given the command, General Roosevelt Jr. and his men waited off the shore of Omaha Beach for the order to start the assault, but he was told to wait. After several verbal requests and one written request (which was later approved), on June 6, 1944, Roosevelt Jr. turned to his men and said, "We'll start the war from right here."[116] Storming the beach with his men from a landing craft, Roosevelt Jr. had his cane in one hand and an army-issued 45.-caliber pistol the other. He ignored the heavy fire, rallied his men and led them into the enemy's line. While on the beach, he organized a group of his men to blast a seawall to allow the advancing allied troops better mobility into German lines. Roosevelt Jr., at the age of fifty-six, was the oldest man and the only general to storm Omaha Beach in the first wave of troops.

A month after his successful campaign, Roosevelt died from a heart attack on July 12, 1944, in Normandy, where his younger brother had died twenty-six years earlier on July 14, 1918. His bravery and courage were later recognized, and he was awarded the Medal of Honor on September 28, 1944. Following the end of the war, the controversy to bring Roosevelt Jr.'s body home for a stateside burial heated up. The family was divided, but Roosevelt's widow, Eleanor Butler Roosevelt, insisted that they leave her husband buried in France. Eleanor argued, "It is more dignified to allow the ones who died in combat to remain in their current military cemeteries."[117] To immortalize his bravery, the Village of Oyster Bay constructed a new library and named it Theodore Roosevelt Jr. Memorial Library.

Despite the prestigious honor that comes with receiving the medal, the benefits outside of being honored in the names of parks is limited. The only benefits Charles Shea, Joseph Schafer and Anthony Casamento received while they were alive was a $200-a-month tax-free pension and a special license plate issued by the State of New York. But the true benefit of receiving the Medal of Honor was knowing that their contributions furthered an American cause and saved the lives of thousands of their fellow soldiers.

9

DEMOBILIZATION AND THE
CHALLENGES TO COME

The May 8, 1945 victory in Europe came after Germany's unconditional surrender, but the war in Pacific was still being waged. The plans for a large-scale invasion of Japan created a final push for mobilization, but after the dropping of two atomic bombs, one on Hiroshima (August 6) and the other on Nagasaki (August 9), Japanese officials surrendered. The bombs leveled important Japanese manufacturing hubs and killed an estimated 200,000 people. The dropping of these bombs made the world gasp and changed global warfare forever.

A large part of the development of the atomic bomb was birthed from Einstein's brainstorming with his friends at his Nassau Point home in Peconic years prior. The second large component of the development of the bomb came from the monitoring and stunting of the Nazi's development an atomic bomb. This work was carried out based on the intelligence gathered by the FBI radio surveillance center in Wadding River. The notes, discussions among other notable scientists and intelligence gathered from the FBI's surveillance of Nazi movement of uranium and heavy water paved the way for Robert Oppenheimer to succeed in the Manhattan Project.

During one successful detonation of the atomic bomb, it was observed that the fireball burned at 7,726 degrees Celsius, the same temperature as the surface of the sun. In response, Oppenheimer stated in disbelief, "Now, I am become death, the destroyer of worlds." The events of August 6 and 9 caused Japanese officials to share this sentiment—that the American war machine was the destroyer of worlds, a force that could not be defeated. This led to the Japanese announcement of surrender on August 14, 1945, and a later formal surrender on September 2, 1945, aboard the USS *Missouri*.

The day after the announcement, August 15, 1945, all the stores were ordered to be closed in most of the towns in Long Island. Shopkeepers in downtowns across Long Island posted signs in their windows that read "closed for peace." In Long Beach, a lawn party was organized to serve food and drinks, but it was later expanded to a beach party at night. Villages like Amityville, Deer Park and Floral Park planned multiday celebrations, with feasts, fireworks, parades and prayer services to remember the soldiers who paid the ultimate sacrifice. In an address, mayor Frederick Heidtmann of Floral Park stated, "We are proud of the 48 boys from our town that died in the war. I do not like to think of this day as a victory. That sounds as if we had gone and conquered, but we did protect our people from aggressors—Hitler and the Japanese. We have gone out in the name of God and brought these people to their knees."[118] Elected town officials across Long Island started an unofficial competition to see which hamlet or village could construct the best veterans' memorials in community squares or gardens.

Following the announcements of the local celebrations, war plants put all their workers on a V-J Holiday. Spokespeople for the collective groups of war plants, such as Ranger Aircraft, Sperry Gyroscope Company, Grumman, Columbian, Liberty Aircraft and Republic Aircraft, stated that there would be no layoffs, that everyone would return to work after enjoying the holiday at home with their communities and families. But across the country, these war manufacturing holidays were more than paid days of celebration; they were days for the managers of the plants to assess the size, profitability and effectiveness of their workforces. A few days after the announcement of the holiday and the promises of no layoffs, Republic notified all their workers not to return to work until they were notified by management. The carefully groomed work environment that once fostered family-friendly take-your-kids-to-work days, sports teams to compete against other plants, daycares and employee-of-the-month awards started to be dismantled.

The first things to go were the daycare centers, which had once allowed single mothers to work. Based on a survey by the United States Department of Labor, "Women Workers in War Production, Their Postwar Employment Plans," 75 percent of all the female defense plant employees surveyed believed they would remain employed after the war. Further details in the Department of Labor study revealed that 86 percent of women wanted to remain employed in defense manufacturing. For Black women, 94 percent on those surveyed planned to continue working in the same field. In a letter to President Harry Truman, former Grumman Aircraft worker Ottile Juliet Gattuss of Lynbrook pleaded:

> *The only jobs to women are office jobs, which pay an average wage of $20 to $22 a week. I am a widow with a mother and a son to support and no other means of income. I pay $45 a month for rent, exclusive of my gas and lights, and at the present time, there is no cheaper place to rent on the entire Long Island. Those being the conditions, I am unable to manage on a $22 a week salary. But my reason for writing to you is not for pity, but I would like to know why, after serving a company in good faith for over three years, it is now impossible to obtain employment with them. I am a lathe hand and was classified as a skilled laborer, but simply because I happen to be a woman, I am not wanted. Won't you kindly look into these matters and consider that a woman can be the head of a family and get as much of an even break as the men.*[119]

The gains made by women in the workforce were gradually erased, as 20,000 women across Long Island were laid off from their jobs. By the end of August 1945, over 5 million defense plant workers across the country were laid off. Within months, the fair wages of the World War II defense manufacturing economy fell in the face of a labor glut. Further escalating the unemployment problem, Nassau County was in a scrabble to find new uses for smaller defense plant properties, which had mostly been abandoned by November 1945. This sense of urgency came from a desire to get these properties back on the county tax rolls. Many were rezoned for residential use.

The plants that survived the end of the war were Liberty, Republic, Sperry and Grumman Aircraft Manufacturing. These companies stayed in business but reduced their workforces to a fraction of the size they had been prior to the end of the war. With the economic fallout on Long Island and in other manufacturing-based communities, President Harry Truman expressed optimism in his speeches. Truman explained that the economic setbacks were due to transitioning from a war-based economy to a peacetime economy.

The abandonment of small-scale wartime manufacturing plants was not the only hardship Long Island faced as it went through demobilization. The gains made in maritime safety in the last decade were in jeopardy. Off the coast of Fire Island, throughout the last century and a half, the shipping route that traversed the South Shore had been nicknamed the Graveyard of the

Atlantic. During World War II, the United States Coast Guard expanded its bases and manpower to prevent Nazi submarine attacks, and it also formed an effective lifesaving force for distressed ships. The debate over whether the Coast Guard was part of federal law enforcement and essential in peacetime or part of the military armed forces played out across Long Island, as local municipalities demanded the bases remain staffed.

Despite the pleas, four bases were closed, including the Lone Hill, Blue Point, Point O' Woods and Smith Point. The largest of all the closed stations was the Tiana Station in Quogue. This station was manned by an all-Black unit throughout the duration of the war and had provided a stringent watch over the South Shore. The Fire Island station, which was the largest during the war (staffed by 125 men for twenty-four hours a day), was down to 8 men in April 1946. The Jones Beach Station, once a hub during the war, was reduced to 1 person, and there were plans to phase out the station altogether. These reductions concerned locals, as Fire Island had 203 calls for help yearly, and Jones station had 118. The alternative to reducing the number of staff due to the large-scale demobilization of guardsmen was to reorganize a Coast Guard auxiliary. These auxiliary forces were made up of local citizens and became the most effective way to fill the needed manpower. This civilian force saved the Moriches Station from closure.

In total, just under 1 million New Yorkers served in the military during World War II. From that total, 43,254 were killed in either the European or Pacific theaters of war. Hundreds of New Yorkers were declared missing in action, but there was no success in recovering them from prisoner of war camps or any of their remains from the battlefields; many were declared dead the year after the war ended. An estimated fifty New Yorkers died in either concertation camps, death camps or prisoner of war camps in Europe or the Pacific. The soldiers who died in these camps were argued to be underreported, but the large-scale records of death and large mass burials made getting an exact number a challenge.

The end of the war created a four-way split of Germany between England, France, the Soviet Union and America. This divided Germany required a large occupying force, but an overwhelming number of soldiers were slated to go home. Demobilizing an army of 3.1 million soldiers came with many challenges and concerns. With the nation's soldiers coming home, they brought with them the eyewitness accounts of 85 million or 3 percent of the world's population dying in either Europe or in the Pacific. According to the Veterans Administration (VA) 37 percent of the soldiers who came home after World War II received psychiatric assistance. The second-largest issue facing America after the war was a postwar recession within most of the nation's industries. Having soldiers adjust to civilian life had to be a priority. The Servicemen's Readjustment Act of 1944, otherwise known as the G.I. Bill, had its first major test between the years of 1945 and 1950. This bill provided funding for veterans to attend college or some type of training program, buy homes with no money down and accept weekly wages of twenty dollars until they found employment.

With the slow demobilization efforts and a federal plan for the transition of soldiers, women across the country and Long Island organized a "Bring Back Daddy Club." The objective of this organization was to apply political pressure at all legislative levels to bring the soldiers home faster. By late 1945, the War Department announced that it would start sending 250,000 to 500,000 soldiers home a month. During the war, New York City ports shipped over 3 million soldiers into combat, and after the war, they brought over 3 million soldiers home. When demobilizing, the impact on newlyweds reshaped the traditional family through unintended consequences. Two out of three wartime marriages ended in divorce before 1950, increasing the national divorce rate by 85 percent.

In December 1945, Congress increased the G.I. Bill's real estate loan guarantee from $4,000 to $8,000. This change in the G.I. Bill and the large influx of returning soldiers created an increased demand in low-cost housing. Throughout the Northeast, Long Island was thought to be an ideal location for new low-cost housing, as it was close to New York City and had surplus land from shuttered defense plants and farms that were forced to sell due to an infestation of golden nematode worms, which devastated Long Island's cash crop, the potato. Prior to World War II, the construction of the Southern State and Northern State Parkways connected Nassau and Suffolk Counties to the city and allowed residents to travel by car instead of public transportation. All of these factors paved the way for the modern Long Island.

Developers, such as Walter Shirley William Zeckendorf and Levitt and Sons, utilized the existing parkways to design suburbs and commerce around the accessibility of the car. Alfred Levitt and William Levitt of Levitt and Son purchased 1,200 acres of land from Island Trees Farm and a surrounding estate for an estimated $300 per acre. The old estate land was purchased from the Merllion Corporation, which was originally owned by Alexander Turner Stewart, the developer of Garden City. The Island Trees land was formerly a potato farm, but it became quarantined due to a golden nematode outbreak. The developers would apply the model of assembly-line production to home construction by shipping prefabricated sections of homes to the construction site and having workers assemble them. This method set a record, allowing them to build thirty-six houses a day.

The Levitt houses started at eight hundred square feet on concrete slabs and came in either a cape or ranch style. The homes included built-in televisions, washers and dryers, built-in kitchen appliances and optional car ports. The homes came in five colors but were mostly identical to each other. Each home had a small backyard for hosting children's play dates or BBQs. The largest developments constructed by Levitt and Son included the Levittowns of Nassau County and Pennsylvania. The Levittown developments were built around public pools, parks, schools, churches and small-scale strip malls, and they all had access to major highways. The roads in Levittowns were constructed on a curve for the dual purpose

Alfred Levitt, the developer of Levittown. He applied a model of assembly-line home construction by shipping prefabricated sections of homes to the site of his community and having workers assemble them. *Courtesy of the Nassau County Photograph Archive.*

of enforcing a slower speed limit and maximizing the greatest number of houses to be built on a block. The communities were marketed as family-friendly for the average suburban family. Another marketable feature of these communities was that they were just twenty-five miles from Manhattan, ten miles from the Queens-Nassau border and close to the Bethpage and Hicksville Train Stations.

By 1951, 17,447 homes had been constructed on the Island Trees Farm land and the surrounding property, which made up parts of the towns of Levittown, Wantagh, Hicksville and Westbury. A two-bedroom house within these communities retailed, on average, for $6,900 in 1947. Due to the increase of demand, the price was raised by $1,000, to $7,990, by the early 1950s. This price point was also based on Congress's revision to the G.I. Bill, which increased loan guarantees in the newly created VA loans. As a result, Nassau County's population increased from 672,765 in 1950 to 1,300,171 in 1960, and Suffolk County's would increase from 276,129 in 1950 to 666,784 in 1960. The townships within Suffolk, such as Babylon, which was mostly a farming-based town, experienced the fastest and largest growth. The population of Babylon went from 45,556 in 1950 to 142,309 in 1960.

Surrounding these developments were strip malls and malls, which made these communities shopping destinations and generated tax revenue for the county and local towns. These new retail businesses and service industries filled the lost revenue from the smaller defense plants that went out of business after the end of the war, and they would compromise 40 percent of Long Island's school tax revenue. This revenue from commercial taxes would later enhance the quality of education for students zoned in schools near or in shopping districts. For most of the 125 school districts across Long Island, the commercial revenue, which was generated by walkable downtowns, was now being generated by shopping centers designed around automobile convenience. While the commerce shifted away from village centers, the once-vibrant nineteenth-century downtown area that was the pride of most communities became abandoned, blighted as tax liabilities.

Above and opposite: By 1951, 17,447 homes had been constructed on this land and the surrounding property, which comprised parts of Levittown, Wantagh, Hicksville and Westbury. These pictures include aerial and road views of the completed development of Island Tree plots. *Courtesy of the Nassau County Photograph Archive.*

Veterans, excited by the chance to buy a Levitt house with no down payment, camped out in front of the Levitt and Sons office to secure a home. Levitt advertised in all media publications throughout the tristate area that home applications would be processed based on each veteran's preference. But what was left out in these advertisements and interviews was he only meant White veterans. Levitt and Son barred Black families from renting homes and racially steered Black families away from buying their homes. The allies of Levitt and Son included local banks, which refused to provide or process VA mortgages to Black veterans who were seeking houses in Levitt developments. This newly designed postwar suburb had the relic of institutionalized segregation that was bestowed by the Ku Klux Klan decades prior. Many of the Klan members of the 1920s worked in the home repair businesses, were bank owners and owned insurance companies. Many civil rights groups claimed the old Klan did not disappear but transformed in the early 1950s; they traded in their white garments for suits and became developers.[120] The new racial ideology was not centered on the inferiority of other races, but it became an argument of economics through real estate values. Levittown's lease clause twenty-six stated, "The tenant agrees not to permit the premises to be used or occupied by any person other than members of the Caucasian race, but the employment and maintenance of other than Caucasian domestic servants shall be permitted." This clause was enforced through evictions and steep fines to the landlords.

Donald Archer, a Black man, and his mother, Myrtle Archer, of Jamaica, Queens, tried to buy a house in Levittown in early 1953. Donald, a veteran, would have been approved for any VA loan, as he had the required income, had he been White. When they went into the sales office, they were told that they were "not selling to Negros at this time." Their case was taken to court with the legal justification that the supreme court banned housing discrimination in any development receiving FHA funds in 1949, but it was ignored in all local district courts. In an interview with *Newsday*, a spokesman for Levittown stated, "Our policy as to whom we sell or do not sell is the same as that of any other builder in the entire Metropolitan area." These racial restrictions were the foundations of the second American civil rights movement.

Nationally, an estimated 1.2 million Black Americans served during World War II, with the guiding idea that they were ending tyranny. However, on returning home, Black veterans all over country and on Long Island found the same conditions they endured prior to the war. Fighting tyranny abroad did not extend to ending racial oppression at home.[121] Returning

Black troops demanded equality and wanted the ideal American dream that returning White soldiers were given. Mortgage lending, quality schools, fair and equal employment and anything that would provide a pathway to the middle class were Black veterans' collective guiding ideas for the second civil rights movement. The local civil rights leaders of the 1950s were all rejected from buying homes in Levittown.

Eugene Burnett, once he received his honorable discharge, got a job as a Suffolk County police officer. Once he was comfortable in his new job, he took himself and his wife to look at a home in Levittown. Once there, the sales manager told him that they were "not selling to negros at this time."[122] Angered by this, Eugene went on to continue his house search. In 1959, he found a home in Wheatly Heights, Suffolk County. When purchasing the house, Eugene left his Suffolk Police squad car in the driveway and moved into the home in middle of the night. Due to threats he received from the neighbors, even after they knew he was a police officer, Eugene slept by the front door of his home with a loaded shotgun, as he feared his house would be burned down. This experience mobilized Eugene to become a key member of the NAACP.

Another Black veteran who was rejected from buying a house in Levittown was Irwin Quintyne. Like Eugene, Irwin was honorably discharged and was looking to use the G.I. Bill, but he was told by Levittown sales managers that they were "not selling to Negros at this time."[123] This anger mobilized Quintyne as well, as was demonstrated through his leadership of the Congress of Racial Equality (CORE).

These boundaries were finally broken when another Black veteran, William Cotter, was evicted from Levittown in 1953, after a White friend signed the lease for his family. After his case was taken to the highest level of the state supreme court, Cotter was permitted to rent and later buy a home in the development in 1959.

The assassination of Martin Luther King Jr. came with more media attention toward local racist policies. In an effort to fix the negative media coverage, Levitt and Son took full page advertisements out in local papers, announcing a policy to develop integration within their developments.

Disgusted as to how local soldiers were being rejected from buying homes in Levittown, developer and veteran Thomas Romano set out to model a just post–World War II society. In North Amityville, between Sunrise Highway and Southern State Parkway, Romano found a 147-acre underutilized farm that was owned by the Purdy family. On this site, Romano built his proposed one-thousand-home development. The set price for a home in Romano's

JOB NO. 1574

Lease dated January 21st, 1948, between ISLAND TREES CORP., a New York Corporation, located at 3230 Northern Boulevard, Manhasset, New York, as Landlord,

LEVITTOWN CORPORATION

and **Herbert Cantor, residing at 170 E. Broadway, Long Beach, New York,** as Tenant.

The Landlord leases to the Tenant premises at Island Trees, Hicksville, N. Y., known by street number as **41 Lilac Lane** for a term commencing on **February 1st, 1948**, and expiring on **January 31st, 1949**, for residential occupancy by the Tenant and the Tenant's immediate family upon the following conditions and covenants:

1. The Tenant agrees to pay rent at the annual rate of $720.00, payable $60.00 monthly in advance on the first day of each month.

2. The Tenant agrees to take good care of the premises and of the household equipment furnished therewith, and forthwith at the Tenant's expense to make all repairs thereto not necessitated by the Landlord's fault, except that the Landlord, at its expense, will make all major structural repairs to the premises not necessitated by the Tenant's fault or that of the Tenant's family, employees, invitees or licensees. The Tenant agrees to deliver up the premises and equipment in good condition at the expiration of the term.

3. The Tenant agrees not to assign this lease or underlet the premises or any part thereof.

4. The Tenant agrees to allow the Landlord to enter the premises at all reasonable hours to examine the same or make repairs.

5. The Tenant agrees that the Landlord shall be exempt from liability for any damage or injury to person or property except such as may be caused by its negligence.

6. The Tenant agrees that this lease shall be subordinate to any mortgages now or hereafter on the premises.

7. The Tenant agrees to comply with all of the statutes, ordinances, rules, orders, regulations and requirements of the Federal, State and Municipal Governments, Departments and Bureaus, applicable to the premises.

8. The Tenant agrees not to do, bring or keep or to permit to be done, brought or kept on the premises anything which will in any way increase the rate of fire insurance thereon.

9. THE TENANT HAS DEPOSITED WITH THE LANDLORD THE SUM OF $100.00 AS SECURITY FOR THE PERFORMANCE OF THIS LEASE, WHICH SUM WITHOUT INTEREST SHALL BE RETURNED TO THE TENANT AFTER THE EXPIRATION OF THE TERM HEREIN PROVIDED THE TENANT HAS FULLY PERFORMED. THE TENANT AGREES NOT TO ASSIGN OR ENCUMBER THE SECURITY.

10. The Tenant agrees that the failure of the Landlord to insist upon a strict performance of any of the conditions and covenants herein shall not be deemed a waiver of any rights or remedies that the Landlord may have, and shall not be deemed a waiver of any subsequent breach or default in the conditions and covenants herein contained. This instrument may not be changed, modified or discharged orally.

11. The Tenant agrees that should the premises or any part thereof be condemned for public use, this lease, at the option of the Landlord, shall become null and void upon the date of taking and rent shall be apportioned as of such date. No part of any award, however, shall belong to the Tenant.

12. The Tenant agrees that if, upon the expiration of the term, the Tenant fails to remove any property belonging to the Tenant, such property shall be deemed abandoned by the Tenant and shall become the property of the Landlord.

13. The Tenant agrees to waive all rights to trial by jury in any summary proceedings hereafter instituted by the Landlord against the Tenant in respect to the premises or in any action brought to recover rent or damages hereunder.

14. The Tenant agrees that the obligation of the Tenant to pay rent and perform all of the other conditions and covenants hereof shall not be affected by the Landlord's inability, because of circumstances beyond its control, to supply any service or to make any repairs or to supply any equipment or fixtures.

15. The Tenant agrees to employ and pay the garbage and rubbish collector designated by the Landlord, in default of which the Landlord may make such payment and charge the same to the Tenant as additional rent.

16. The Tenant agrees that the premises are being rented "as is" and that the Landlord shall not be obligated to make any alterations, improvements or renovations therein, nor any repairs other than those expressly provided for herein.

17. THE TENANT AGREES TO ASSUME THE RESPONSIBILITY OF ENSURING THAT NO PERSON SHALL WALK AND NOTHING SHALL BE PLACED UPON THE UNFINISHED SECTION OF THE ATTIC FLOOR AND THAT IN THE EVENT THIS CONDITION IS VIOLATED AND DAMAGE RESULTS TO SUCH ATTIC FLOOR AND/OR TO THE CEILING BELOW, THE TENANT WILL PAY UPON DEMAND AS ADDITIONAL RENT THE COST OF REPAIRS WHICH ARE ESTIMATED AT A MINIMUM OF $60.00.

18. The Tenant agrees that the Landlord assumes no obligation for the servicing or repair of the oil burner, washing machine, cooking stove, refrigerator, or ventilating fan installed in the premises. Solely for the convenience of the Tenant, the Landlord has made the following arrangements, for the carrying out of which, however, the Landlord shall not be held responsible:

> The oil burner parts are represented by the manufacturer as guaranteed for one year.
>
> If and so long as the Tenant purchases fuel oil from Live Heat, Inc., it is represented by that Company that the oil burner will be serviced without charge.
>
> Bruno-New York, Inc., represents that the washing machine will be serviced without charge for one year.
>
> The manufacturer of the cooking stove represents that its parts are guaranteed for one year but no service is to be provided.
>
> The manufacturer of the refrigerator represents that it will be serviced for one year.
>
> The ventilator is not guaranteed at all nor will there be any servicing of it.

19. The Landlord will furnish at its own expense water consumed on the premises in reasonable quantities for ordinary domestic and gardening purposes.

20. The Tenant agrees not to erect or permit to be erected any fence, either fabricated or growing, upon any part of the premises.

21. The Tenant agrees not to keep or permit to be kept any animals, pigeons or fowl upon the premises except not more than two domestic animal pets.

22. The Tenant agrees not to install or permit to be installed any laundry poles or lines outside of the house, except that one portable revolving laundry dryer, not more than seven feet high, may be used in the rear yard on days other than Saturdays, Sundays and legal holidays, provided that such dryer shall be removed from the outside when not in actual use on such permitted days.

23. The Tenant agrees not to place or permit to be placed any garbage or rubbish outside of the house except in a closed metal receptacle located to the rear of the kitchen door and not more than one foot from the exterior of the house and except when placed at the curbline before removal in accordance with the regulations of the collecting agency.

24. THE TENANT AGREES NOT TO RUN OR PARK OR PERMIT TO BE RUN OR PARKED ANY MOTOR VEHICLE UPON ANY PART OF THE PREMISES.

25. THE TENANT AGREES TO CUT OR CAUSE TO BE CUT THE LAWN AND REMOVE OR CAUSE TO BE REMOVED TALL GROWING WEEDS AT LEAST ONCE A WEEK BETWEEN APRIL FIFTEENTH AND NOVEMBER FIFTEENTH IN EACH YEAR. UPON THE TENANT'S FAILURE THE LANDLORD MAY DO SO AND CHARGE THE COST THEREOF TO THE TENANT AS ADDITIONAL RENT.

26. THE TENANT AGREES NOT TO PERMIT THE PREMISES TO BE USED OR OCCUPIED BY ANY PERSON OTHER THAN MEMBERS OF THE CAUCASIAN RACE BUT THE EMPLOYMENT AND MAINTENANCE OF OTHER THAN CAUCASIAN DOMESTIC SERVANTS SHALL BE PERMITTED.

27. The Tenant agrees not to place or permit to be placed upon the premises any sign whatsoever except a family or professional name or address plate whose size, style and location are first approved in writing by the Landlord.

28. The Terant agrees not to use or permit the premises to be used for any purpose other than as a private dwelling for one family or as a professional office of a physician or dentist resident therein.

29. The Tenant agrees not to erect or permit to be erected on the premises any building or structure, or to make or permit to be made any alterations or additions to the premises, or paint or permit to be painted the exterior of the house other than in the original color, unless appropriate plans, specifications and/or colors are first approved in writing by the landlord.

30. The Tenant agrees not to do or permit to be done on the premises anything of a disreputable nature, or constituting a nuisance, or tending to impair the condition or appearance of the premises, or tending to interfere unreasonably with the use and enjoyment of other premises by other Tenants.

31. The Tenant agrees that, if default be made in the performance of any of the conditions or covenants herein, or if the premises shall become vacant or if the Tenant shall file a petition in bankruptcy or be adjudicated a bankrupt or make an assignment for the benefit of creditors, the Landlord may (A) re-enter the premises by force, summary proceedings or otherwise, and remove all persons therefrom, without being liable to prosecution therefor, and the Tenant hereby expressly waives the service of any notice in writing of intention to re-enter, or (B) the Landlord may terminate this lease on giving to the Tenant 5 days' notice in writing of its intention so to do, and this lease shall expire on the date fixed for the expiration hereof. Such notice may be given by mail to the Tenant addressed to the premises. The Tenant agrees, in either event, to pay at the same times as the rent is payable hereunder a sum equivalent to such rent; and the Landlord may rent the premises on behalf of the Tenant, (for a period of time beyond the original expiration date of this lease, if it so elects), without releasing the Tenant from any liability, applying any moneys collected, first to the expense of resuming or obtaining possession, second to the restoration of the premises to a rentable condition, and then to the payment of the rent and all other charges due and to become due to the Landlord, any surplus to be paid to the Tenant who shall remain liable for any deficiency.

32. The Landlord agrees that the Tenant on performing the conditions and covenants aforesaid shall and may peacefully and quietly have, hold and enjoy the premises for the term aforesaid.

33. It is mutually agreed that the conditions and covenants contained in this lease shall be binding upon the parties hereto and upon their respective successors, heirs, executors, administrators and assigns.

IN WITNESS WHEREOF, the Landlord has caused these presents to be signed by its proper corporate officer and caused its proper corporate seal to be hereto affixed and the Tenant has hereunto set his hand and seal.

LEVITTOWN CORPORATION
XXXXXXXXXXXXXXXX.

By: *Will Ope*
Authorized Officer

Herbert Cantor   L. S.

NO NOTICES WILL BE MAILED. RENT IS DUE AND PAYABLE ON THE FIRST OF EACH MONTH AT THE OFFICE IN THE ISLAND TREES COMMUNITY.

Opposite and above: Levittown's rent with the option to buy was the way to home ownership for thousands of people. Clause twenty-six, as seen in these images, stated, "The tenant agrees not to permit the premises to be used or occupied by any person other than members of the Caucasian race, but the employment and maintenance of other than Caucasian domestic servants shall be permitted." *Courtesy of Levittown Library's historical achieves.*

Black soldiers coming home were the cornerstones of the 1950s and 1960s civil rights movement because, in defeating oppression in the war, they inspired a want for a more just society in America. Pictured are Eugene Burnett and Richard Coles; Eugene later became a key member of the NAACP. *Courtesy of the Eugene Barnett collection.*

Roneck Park was $6,990. Each home was marketed as being "dedicated to the proposition that all men are created equal." Veterans were automatically approved for no-money-down, thirty-year mortgages with monthly payments of $44.60. Unfortunately, the community of Roneck Park did not provide the integrated societal vision of Thomas Romano, but it did become a staple for activism within the civil rights movement. The community produced leaders such Dr. Eugene Reed of the NAACP and fueled the Hollywood Baptist Church and Bethel AME Church of Amityville to organize civil rights marches and sit-ins both nationally and locally. The community hosted political icons such as Thurgood Marshall and Eleanor Roosevelt, who both gave discussions on civil rights challenges and national human rights struggles in the northern suburbs.

With the civil rights struggles that were being encountered throughout Long Island by many Black demobilized veterans, a symbol for world peace and human rights was constructed in Lake Success. The shuttered Sperry plant lay vacant in the village of Lake Success, and local officials were eager to get it back on the tax rolls. In April 1946, Lake Success mayor P. Schuyler VanBloem met with a search committee from the United Nations. The group was eager to find a headquarters for the United Nations, and Mayor VanBloem promised them a community that would embrace the ideals of the global organization. On August 29, 1946, the United Nations Building was opened, and held its first session there.

The first session included 1,500 delegates from around the world who descended on the small village of 700 people. The optimism of the locals for becoming global citizens and having this symbol of global peace and security in their backyard lasted for a little over two years. In late 1948,

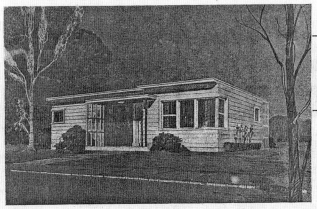

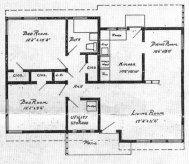
Builder Thomas Romano purchased 147 acres of land in North Amityville for the construction of over one thousand homes. The marketing of these homes was centered on resisting the "undemocratic restrictions of race, color or creed." This development became known as Ronek Park. *Courtesy of the Historic Photograph and Postcard Collection of the Town of Babylon, Office of Historic Services.*

atomic energy was being developed as a means of peace to offer a rebuttal to the destruction of the atomic bombs. At the United Nations Atomic Energy Commission at Lake Success, negotiations broke down over whether to veto the peaceful use of atomic energy plants. The United States blamed the USSR for expanding atomic energy aggressively, and the USSR argued that America was attempting to put all atomic bombs under its own guidelines with no accountability to any other country. This stalemate that played out was the dawning of the Cold War. In less than a year, on August 29, 1949, the USSR successfully tested an atomic bomb, which was the official start of the Cold War.

Once a symbol of optimism, the Lake Success UN Building was pressured to move. The introduction of the Cold War reversed the town's desire for global citizenry through promoting peace. Citizens were tested on their level of American patriotism through their defensiveness against any potential communist ideology. Levittown developments across Long Island installed clauses in leases that enforced the evictions of "public nuisances"; these clauses were used to purge the development of suspected communists. Throughout Long Island, large-scale defense plants that had previously scaled back their workforces started to expand their production of war planes and other pieces of armory in the anticipation that a war may come. In a sign of the changing culture, Sperry Gyroscope Company purchased its old manufacturing plant in Lake Success back from the federal government, which was renting it out to the United Nations. In October 1950, Sperry officially canceled its lease to the United Nations, stating, "America is under the threatening shadow of another global conflict, the company needed more space to produce equipment for national defense."[124] As it had done five years prior, in 1950, Republic Aircraft innovated its production line at an amazing speed and began producing 7,524 Republic F-84 Thuderjets for the United States Airforce, and Grumman built 1,382 F9F Panthers to monitor activities in the growing communist theater in the Pacific.

Long Island once again militarized and mobilized for the conflicts to come; the introduction of ninety thousand defense manufacturing jobs carried the region's economy until the late 1980s. The old Camp Upton military base reinvented itself as Brookhaven National Labs in 1947. With the recognition of all the horrors of a nuclear fallout, the top project at the lab was to split atoms and find multiple uses for nuclear reactions. Postwar optimism in America for global peace and a more just society shifted to pessimism of a likely war as a priority. The eagerness for soldiers coming home from a brutal and traumatizing war to a long-lasting peace switched to war anxiety that fueled the widespread construction of home bomb shelters.

History defined the collective dynamism of World War II as the base that forged modern America. This modern America not only built suburbia but also propelled the average American town into global citizenry. However, it also drew lines created obstacles and challenges that followed its citizens into the twenty-first century. The biases, beliefs and assumptions of prewar America that reinforced racial barriers and ethnic stereotypes after the war were fought in the streets by former soldiers. These veterans who started a front for the civil rights movement had their passions fueled by the potential of what a future America could look like and lessons they witnessed at the hands of brutality and hatred in Europe and the Pacific firsthand. A clear definition of civil rights collided with a population that was fighting to reverse any gains for equality. Economically, America had one of the largest expansions of the middle class, as it broke down the barriers of small-town consumerism to factories and their workers who were producing a global market. Factories across Nassau and Suffolk Counties shipped goods to European and Pacific countries that were struggling to rebuild, and all the local workers had a front seat to witness their rebuilding.

As for the lives lost in the war and how they were immortalized, these will be defined by individual town squares across most of America, which have monuments dedicated to their community's efforts during World War II. But Long Island, unlike most communities, does not need a monument to declare its contributions. Long Island itself is a monument. Its culture, physical landscape, morals and contradictions were all shaped through the spirit of World War II. This legacy, unlike a monument, stands the test of time and allows those who gave the ultimate sacrifice in combat to never die the second death of being forgotten.

NOTES

Introduction: Pre–World War II Long Island

1. H.W. Evans, "Alienism in the Democracy," *Kourier Magazine* 3, no. 8 (July 1927): 12–16.

Defending the Homefront from Threats Outside and Within

2. "Engineer Seized as Spy," *Newsday*, June 30, 1941, 3.
3. Ibid., 11.
4. "Roeder Aided by Jap Agent in Espionage," *Nassau Daily Review-Star*, September 21, 1942, 1.
5. "Nazi Spy, Accused in Trial of Ring Here, Nabbed by FBI," *Nassau Daily Review-Star*, January 15, 1940, 1.
6. "Federal Bureau of Investigation, RE: Investigation into German Bund Activities," April 18, 1938, www.vault.fbi.gov, 22.
7. "40,000 at Nazi Camp Fete," *New York Times*, August 15, 1938.
8. George Dewan, "Long Island: Our Story," *Newsday*, 1998, 238.
9. "Federal Bureau of Investigation, RE: Report on German American Bund," March 16, 1939, www.vault.fbi.gov, 15.
10. "Federal Bureau of Investigation Memorandum for Director, RE: Fritz Kuhn," May 12, 1939, www.vault.fbi.gov, 7.
11. "Federal Bureau of Investigation Memorandum for Director, RE: Fritz Kuhn," April 25, 1939, www.vault.fbi.gov, 3.

12. "Bund Unit and League Settle Camp Dispute," *County Review*, June 26, 1941, 1.
13. "FBI Seizes Nassau Aliens in Big Raid," *Newsday*, December 5, 1942, 1.

FBI Detainees and Counterintelligence

14. John Strausbaugh, *Victory City: A History of New York and New Yorkers During World War II* (New York: Twelve Press, 2018), 247.
15. "Alien Roundup Takes 3 Here," *Nassau Daily Review-Star*, December 9, 1941, 1.
16. "Valianski Is Seen as Key to Spy Ring: Central Islip Waiter Held for Robbery Admits, He Is Gestapo Agent," *County Review*, April 24, 1941, 1.
17. "Federal Bureau of Investigation Memorandum for Director. RE Fritz Ernst Rudloff with Aliases Espionage," March 28, 1942, 5, www.vault.fbi.gov.
18. Raymond Batvinis, "Hoover's Secret War Against Axis Spies: FBI Counterespionage During World War II," University Press of Kansas, 2014, 189.
19. Raymond Batvinis, "Long Island Home's Secret Role in WWII Espionage Revealed," NBC 4 (New York), June 6, 2014, www.fbistudies.com.
20. "Seize 'Nazi Spy' At Camp Upton," *Newsday*, July 1, 1945, 3.
21. Ibid., 1.
22. "Hart Faces Court Martial as Traitor Trained Spy of Nazis," *Newsday*, December 24, 1945, 3.

Civilian Defense

23. "Nassau Goes on War Basis: 4,000 Air Wardens Sought," *Nassau Daily Review-Star*, December 9, 1941, 1.
24. "Retire 2,000 Nassau Airplane Spotters," *Newsday*, October 5, 1943, 5.
25. "Air Wardens Sought," *Newsday*, 1.
26. New York State Archives, "They Also Served: New Yorkers on the Home Front. A Guide to Records of the New York State War Council," 1994, www.archives.nysed.gov, 9.
27. Ibid., 19
28. Sophie Glidden-Lyon, "This Is No Clam Bake: Mayor La Guardia and the Office of Civilian Defense," NYC Department of Records & Information Service, November 16, 2017, www.archives.nyc.
29. "Recruits for Air Warden Duty to Sign Monday," *Long Island News and Owl*, December 12, 1941, 1.

30. "650 Wardens Are Needed for Quota Training Continues," *Long Island News and Owl*, December 26, 1941, 1.

31. "County Blackout Complete: All Lights Out by 10 Minutes After Alarm," *Nassau Daily Review-Star*, March 25, 1942, 1.

32. "100,000 in Civilian Defense Work Here," *Newsday*, April 23, 1942, 5.

Mobilization of Troops

33. "The Text of the Attorney General's Speech," *New York Times*, October 13, 1942, 12.

34. "Regular Army Enlistees Get Aid for Dependents," *Newsday*, November 1, 1945, 9.

35. Jean Horic, "The Draft Bill: I'm Against Draft," *Newsday*, September 6, 1940, 15.

36. "Draft Board Offical Arrested: FBI Charges," *Newsday*, October 17, 1944, 3.

37. "Change Draft Appeal Is Unfair Debunked by Haber," *Newsday*, June 5, 1943, 5.

38. "Women in the Army," *Newsday*, May 25, 1942, 13.

39. Ibid.

40. "WAAC Begins Recruiting Drive Here," *Newsday*, February 25, 1943, 3.

41. "Women, War and Pants," *Newsday*, April 30, 1943, 15.

42. Strausbaugh, *Victory City*, 324.

43. Jean Springer, "Interview with Jean Springer and Interviewer Jeff Miskimens at Cincinnati Ohio," Library of Congress, American Folklife Center, Veterans History Project, November 6, 2007.

44. Christa Kadletz, "Women Pilots Help Win World War II," *Social Science Docket, New York and New Jersey State Councils for Social Studies* 10, no. 2 (Fall 2010): 20.

45. "Plan Sixth Open House to Recruit Student Nurses," *Newsday*, October 16, 1944, 18.

46. "Army Corps Needs 50 More Local Nurses, Medical Auxiliary Hears," *Newsday*, November 2, 1944, 22.

47. "Nassau Nurse Tends Soldier on Airplane Ride for Life," *Newsday*, November 12, 1943, 6.

48. "Nurses Mothers Organize, Sponsored by Red Cross," *Newsday*, March 31, 1944, 10.

49. Nancy Leftenant, "Fallen 66," interview by Richard Gant, August 21, 2012.

50. Merle English, "Pilots Who Broke Race Barrier," *Newsday*, October 8, 1984, 6.

51. Mike Conn, "Glen Cove WWII Vet Remembers Days in the Air: Tuskegee Airmen Recalls World War II," *Long Island Herald*, June 6, 2019, www.liherald.com.

The War Off the Coast of Long Island

52. David Behrens, "Serving on the Home Front: Making Sacrifices on LI, Chapter Seven/Modern Era, Long Island: Our Story," *Newsday*, 1998, 305.
53. "U.S. Acts on U-Boat Scare: Navy Alert," *Newsday*, March 18, 1945, 5.
54. Richard Goldstein and John Cullen, "Coast Guardsman Who Detected Spies, Dies at 90," *New York Times*, September 2, 2011.
55. David Taylor, "The Inside Story of How a Nazi Plot to Sabotage the U.S. War Effort was Foiled," *Smithsonian Magazine*, June 28, 2016, www.smithsonianmag.com.
56. "Nassau Set for Nazi Buzz Bombs," *Newsday*, January 9, 1945, 1.
57. "Lift Hush-Hush from Radio That Put Finger on Nazi Subs," *Newsday*, January 14, 1946, 2.
58. Karen Tyler, "Only One Sub Sunk Anywhere Near LI," *Newsday*, June 18, 1973, 2A.
59. "Fire on Normandie Laid to a Nazi Spy," *New York Times*, November 13, 1947, 9.

Arsenal for Democracy: Wartime Manufacturing

60. "Americans Who Buy Bonds Are Opening the Road, Too," *Nassau Daily Review*, December 12, 1944, 10.
61. "Bond Workers Plan for Nassau," *Nassau Daily Review*, June 2, 1944, 1.
62. "Weller Explains Fuel Oil Ration Urges Conversion," *Long Island News and Owl*, December 11, 1942, 7.
63. "OPA Advises Auto Drivers of Privilege," *Nassau Daily Review-Star*, February 1, 1943, 1.
64. "Trio Arrested for Possession of Gas Stamps," *Nassau Daily Review-Star*, December 12, 1942, 1.
65. "700,000, Pounds of Scrap Tomorrow Is the Local Quota," *Long Island News and Owl*, May 21, 1943, 1.
66. "Salvage Spokesman says Nassau's Stingy with Fat," *Newsday*, August 18, 1943, 6.
67. "1LB Fat Processes 260 Quarts Plasma," *Nassau Daily Review-Star*, March 27, 1945, 7.
68. "January Was Top Month in Salvage Campaign Here," *Newsday*, February 5, 1944, 3.

69. "Pork Despised as Too Fat, Gives Leaf Lard, Home Made Shortening," *Newsday*, March 23, 1944, 28.
70. "2 L.I. Airplane Firms' Earnings Hit Peak in 1939," *Brooklyn Daily Eagle*, March 27, 1940, 23.
71. "Plane Builders Boost Hiring, Survey Shows," *Brooklyn Daily Eagle*, March 3, 1941, 16.
72. "Youth Service Councils Planned," *Newsday*, May 4, 1942, 8.
73. Ken Bartowski, "A Model Aircraft Armada," *New York Archives Magazine*, 2019, 21.
74. "War Work Plan for Schoolchildren," *Newsday*, May 14, 1943, 2.
75. Strausbaugh, *Victory City*, 306.
76. "RVC Resident Testify on War Plant Discrimination," *Newsday*, April 9, 1943, 22.
77. "Grumman Plant Is Seeking Workers," *Port Jefferson Times*, May 28, 1943; "486,100 Women Worked in the Aircraft Industry in Nov. 1943, Compared to 23,100 Women in Jan. 1942 and 28,500 in Oct. 1944," *Aviation Facts and Figures* (Washington, D.C.: American Aviation Publications, 1959), 74.
78. New York State Archives, "They Also Served," 13.
79. "40 Enrolled in New Childcare Course Arranged by Hempstead War Council," *Nassau Daily Review-Star*, May 1, 1942, 17.
80. "Workers Sought at Child Center," *Nassau Daily Review-Star*, February 22, 1943, 18.
81. "Grumman Opens Child Care Home," *Nassau Daily Review-Star*, July 15, 1943, 10.
82. Irene McLaughlin, "Gals by Hundreds Walk Out of This School Right into War Jobs," *Newsday*, November 11, 1942, 3.
83. "Paper in Suit Served, Faust School asks $250,000 from Republic Aviation," *Nassau Daily Review-Star*, May 10, 1941, 5.
84. Joshua Stoff, *Long Island Aircraft Manufacturers*, Images of America (Charleston, SC: Arcadia Publishing, 2010), 63.
85. Erik Eckholm, "10 Feet Below Waters Off Midway Atoll, a Famous Flying Dud," *New York Times*, January 1, 2013.
86. "Grumman's Hellcat Is One of the Lowest Cost Fighter Planes Made," *Wall Street Journal*, June 7, 1944, 6.
87. "Speed Range and Altitude of War Planes Increased by New Development," *Newsday*, March 10, 1944, 13.
88. Anne Petersen, "3 Women Serve as Test Pilots for Navy Hellcats and Avenger," *Newsday*, November 17, 1943, 20.
89. "Grumman Hellcat, Navy's New Fighter Plane, Gets Baptism of Fire in Marcus Island Raid," *Wall Street Journal*, September 10, 1943, 7.

90. "3 Destroyers Sunk by Hellcat Fighters," *New York Times*, September 21, 1944, 4.
91. "'Jumping Joe' Praises Hellcat Builders," *Newsday*, July 1, 1944, 2.
92. "Share Hellcats Glory: 20,000 in Grumman Plant Are Congratulated," *New York Times*, June 26, 1944, 7.
93. "Grumman Leads Nation in Plane Volume," *Newsday*, December 30, 1943, 2.
94. Annual Report 1955 Republic Aviation Corporation, Delaware Corporation, Farmingdale, New York, March 23, 1956, 1.
95. "Thunderbolt Debut Stirs Plant: Republic Workers Hailed as a Success," *Newsday*, May 11, 1943, 5.
96. "Republic Slashes Time, Cost of Thunderbolts," *Newsday*, January 11, 1945, 3.
97. Madline Ryttenberg, "Nassau Sees Robot Bomb-But on Truck: Republic's Answer to Revenge," *New York Times*, January 4, 1945, 2.

POWs Off and On Long Island

98. Matthias Reiss, *Controlling Sex in Captivity: POWs and Sexual Desire in the United States* (New York: Bloomsbury Publishing, 2018), 32.
99. Marie Carlson and Kirk Price, "4 Madmen Flee Hospital," *Newsday*, November 8, 1946, 1.
100. "Army Reveals the Closing Up of Camo Upton," *Nassau Daily Review-Star*, September 1, 1944, 1.
101. "Report from the Swiss Legation About Camp Upton, Aliens Division," April 3, 1942, Longwood Library, Bayles Local History Room, Camp Upton File.
102. Donald Bayles and Paul Infranco, "The History of Camp Upton: World War I Through World War II," Longwood Society for Historic Preservation publication, Middle Island, New York, letter excerpts from POW Josef Kraft, 2017, 169.
103. Kirk Price, "Vets Turned Down While POWs Work at Upton, Goll Says," *Newsday*, December 6, 1945, 3.
104. "Noble—and Dumb," *Newsday*, July 12, 1945, 15.
105. "Says POWs Unneeded Here," *Newsday*, July 13, 1945, 5.
106. "Farm Group Demands POW Labor Now: Hits Red Tape," *Newsday*, July 12, 1945, 5.
107. Michael Colamonico, "Michael Colamonico interview with Joseph Sledge at VA Medical Center," Library of Congress, American Folklife Center, Veterans History Project, November 6, 2007.

108. Ibid.

109. "Red Cross Food Kept POWs Alive in Nazi Camp, Mitchel Flier Says," *Newsday*, March 8, 1949, 17.

110. Andrew Hodge and George Denise, "Behind Nazi Lines: My Father's Heroic Quest to Save 149 World War II POWs," *Berkley Caliber*, 2015, 30.

111. Rhoda Amon, "Long Island: Our Story/Chapter 7: The Modern Era/ Listening for News of the Boys," *Newsday*, May 1998, A43.

112. Wesley Sheffield, "Nazi POWs Leave Here for Occupied Europe," *Newsday*, March 22, 1946, 3.

Medal of Honor Recipients of Long Island

113. Jimmy Carter, "Medal of Honor Remarks on Presenting the Award to Cpl. Anthony Casamento," Jimmy Carter Presidential Library, Folder August 21, 1980, Container 172.

114. "Sergeant Shaefer to Get Honor Medal: Richmond Hill Man Stopped Nazi Attack," *New York Times*, June 7, 1945, 7.

115. Tom Morris, "Long Island Medal of Honor Winning, Long Island: Our Story," *Newsday*, 1998, 311.

116. Stephen Ambrose, *D-Day: June 6, 1944, The Climactic Battle of World War II* (New York: Simon & Schuster, 1995), 500.

117. "Leave War Dead Abroad: Mrs. T.R. Jr.," *Newsday*, September 1947, 7.

Demobilization and the Challenges to Come

118. Staff Writer, "V-J Day Celebration is Observed at Floral Park," *Newsday*, September 4, 1945, 38.

119. Ottilie Gattuss, "Letter to President Harry Truman," Northrop Grumman History Center, Bethpage, New York, September 6, 1945, www.bethpagecommunity.com.

120. Christopher Verga, interview with Eugene Burnett, Wheatly Heights, NY, August 2016.

121. Ibid.

122. Ibid.

123. Christopher Verga, interview with Delores Quintyne, Amityville, NY, July 2016.

124. "Sperry Gyroscope Purchases Its Lake Success Plant from Government," *Newsday*, October 20, 1950, 4.

ABOUT THE AUTHOR

Christopher Verga is an instructor in Long Island history and the foundations of American history at Suffolk Community College, and he is a contributor to the online local news sites Greater Babylon, Greater Bay Shore and Greater Patchogue. His published works include *Civil Rights Movement on Long Island* (Images of America), *Bay Shore* (Images of America) and *Saving Fire Island from Robert Moses*. Christopher has a doctorate degree in education from St. John's University. His dissertation work included studies of Long Island Native Americans and the impact of tribal recognition within their cultural identity.